AGAIN

MAY GOD FORGIVE US!

by

Robert Welch

BELMONT PUBLISHING COMPANY

Publishing history . . . .

Hardbound		*Paperbound*	
June, 1952	*3,000 copies*	*March, 1952*	*25,000 copies*
August, 1952	*3,000 copies*	*May, 1952*	*110,000 copies*
September, 1952	*3,000 copies*	*July, 1952*	*25,000 copies*
October, 1954	*3,000 copies*	*September, 1952*	*25,000 copies*

In magazine format, as one issue of AMERICAN OPINION
January, 1960   *50,000 copies*

The above record applies solely to *May God Forgive Us*. The biographical sketch of Generalissimo Chiang Kai-shek, which is reprinted here as the last part of this small book, was first published as the May, 1957 edition of *One Man's Opinion*, the magazine that later became *American Opinion*. The total printing and sale was probably only about ten thousand copies. (The record has disappeared in the archives, too deep for excavation.) And it has not been reprinted since. But the author retained the copyright to that treatise. He also acquired the copyright to *May God Forgive Us*, by formal assignment from Henry Regnery Company. And this present edition is issued by

Belmont Publishing Company, Belmont, Massachusetts 02178

Table Of Contents

Dedication

"To fear not sensible failure
Nor covet the game at all,
But fighting, fighting, fighting,
Die, driven against the wall."

THE QUARTER of a million brave patriots of Bor-Komorowski's army, mercilessly betrayed by Stalin, died literally driven against the physical walls of their crumbling city of Warsaw. But there are still harder forms of death, in the fight for the very cause rather than the personal enjoyment of freedom, against less material walls.

Behind the Iron Curtain today there are still men and women who, with little hope that they will ever recover freedom for themselves, are daily risking torture and death in their unceasing secret fight against the enveloping darkness of Communism. Without the sustaining excitement of battle, these men and women are willing to buy with their suffering and their lives a tiny breach in the blanket of tyranny. It is to these men and women who, as individuals, are willing even to die, driven against the wall of collectivist suppression, for their very beliefs in the dignity and worth and rights of individual man, that this small book is humbly dedicated.

A Short Prologue

The following chapter of history began exactly twenty years ago as a personal letter. After an incubation period of several months it appeared as a baby book, published by the Henry Regnery Company. During the 1952 political campaigns the book grew rapidly in reach and muscle. In fact, the wide readership of *May God Forgive Us* in Texas, during the last months of the presidential campaign, was given credit by some people for having enabled Eisenhower to carry that state against Adlai Stevenson. Thus proving once again that "man proposes, but God disposes." For nothing could have been further from the intention of the author — who was a Taft man all the way — than to help the man who, as the head of NATO, had already described himself as one-twelfth an American.

Actually, however, we cannot credit the wisdom of God for what took place, but must blame the stupidity of men. For Eisenhower ran with great ostentation as an anti-Communist. In Wisconsin, for instance, he teamed up with, and got the wholehearted support of, Senator Joseph McCarthy — the man whom he later, as President, was to do everything in his power to insult, to hamstring, to undermine, and to destroy. For, during the campaign, anti-Communism fitted the very strong mood of the American people, which *May God Forgive Us* in its small way was helping to make even stronger.

Adlai Stevenson had been picked by the *Insiders* to make a

sacrifice play through running as Eisenhower's opponent, thus causing Eisenhower to show in a far better light. For Stevenson's pro-Communist leanings were pretty well known to everybody. While the far more extensive, more effective, more continuous, and more treasonous activities of Eisenhower on behalf of the Communist advance, throughout his whole career, was still one of the most successfully suppressed secrets in all human history. And it is worth noting in passing that Stevenson fully understood the role he had been obliged to play. He even remarked at one point that it only hurt for a while.

It is also worth noting that this whole maneuver was in accordance with a brazen bit of strategy which the Communists use over and over. Whenever a revulsion against the power and progress of Communism starts to gather enough steam to become dangerous to the plans of the top Conspirators, they are already prepared to have one of their own men run around to the front of the opposing forces and lead this crusade against themselves. The opposition can then be gradually and cleverly led astray and dissipated, or sometimes even cunningly steered into the service of the Conspiracy.

And it is – or should be – amazing how repeatedly the public falls into this same trap, always digging its future grave deeper before it climbs out to daylight once again. After taking eight years to realize that Eisenhower was using the full power and prestige of the Presidency to help the Communists all he dared, both abroad and here at home, the American people were ready in just eight more years to be deceived once more in identically the same way, by another pseudo-Conservative named Richard Nixon.

Among those thus deceived, and who worked hardest for Nixon's election, were many staunch anti-Communists who ought to have known better. Because, for those who had done their homework properly, the real Nixon record was unmistakably clear. The Blue Book of The John Birch Society, to give one illustration, had exposed the crafty character of Richard Nixon when it was first published in 1959. There were many other sources for the record that had earned him the sobriquet of Tricky Dick. As early as 1947, soon after he had first gone to Congress — and while he was still riding the anti-Communist wave which put him there, which got him reelected in 1948, and which enabled him to defeat Helen Gahagan Douglas for a Senate seat in 1950 — Nixon was already hard at work feathering his nest in the unlighted Communist grove.

And he was already associating closely with such veteran pro-Communists as Christian Herter, Henry Cabot Lodge, and Earl Warren, in some of their behind-the-scenes activities. Always a daring gambler, Nixon used his anti-Communist pose and pretenses — even his grossly exaggerated part in the exposure of Alger Hiss — as a brilliant gambit in the political game. He expected it not only to enable him to win his early contests for higher and higher office, but to pay fabulous dividends at some time in the future, when the *Insiders* realized that he was really on their side but the public still did not. And this calculated risk has certainly proved immensely successful.

In fact, it is one revelation of supreme hypocrisy on the part of President Nixon which now gives timeliness to the present reprinting of the treatise that follows. His recently announced plan to pay a visit of state to the infinitely cruel, murderous, bestial and lying regime which holds the population of mainland China enslaved by torture and terror, is not only an almost unbelievable repudiation of the campaign promises on which he was elected, but is an unqualified and unforgivable betrayal of the American people. It should prompt many patriotic citizens to look at that long and original betrayal of the Chinese people into the hands of these monsters at Peking, by our government, which was fully outlined in *May God Forgive Us* just twenty years ago.

For much has happened, and many things have changed on the surface of this suffering globe, during those twenty years. But in one area of human activity, unfortunately, there has been no change at all. The heads of *our government* are still doing everything that they dare – as they have now done steadily throughout three decades – to help the Great Conspiracy in its determined and ruthless march toward enslavement of the total population of the earth. And no feature of this treasonous activity could or should bring more shame and more fear to patriotic Americans than the military support, financial support, and moral support which we have given to Mao Tse-tung and Chou En-lai and their fellow criminals over the past twenty-seven years.

So we have pulled a copy of *May God Forgive Us* out of our "permanent files"; added to it our biographical sketch of Chiang Kai-shek, which constituted the whole May, 1957 issue of *One Man's Opinion*; and published this combination as the unpretentious and inexpensive paperback book that you now have before you. Both parts still constitute the very personal kind of message which each of them was when it first appeared. There are a few passages that might be changed in wording, and one conjecture which might be omitted altogether in the light of later knowledge, if the context were being written today. But on the whole both studies, besides being completely free of factual errors, have stood up very well even as correct interpretations of events about which so much so-called "history" has been so terribly and deceptively distorted.

Also, for those who need reassurance about the professional quality or value of literary fare so unprofessionally produced, maybe we can be forgiven the immodesty of quoting just two significant comments. In 1952 General A.C. Wedemeyer, who had been the Commanding Officer of all

American forces in China during some of the period covered, stated of *May God Forgive Us* that it was " . . . the most comprehensive and objective treatment of the complex situation in the Far East that I have yet read." This evaluation appeared on the jacket or cover of all editions published by Regnery. And in 1957 Dr. Hollington Tong, the then Ambassador to the United States from the Republic of China, was kind enough to state publicly that our essay was the best short biography of President Chiang Kai-shek that he had ever read.

One much too flattering foreword about the author, which one of his friends insisted on putting in the original editions of *May God Forgive Us* when published by Regnery, was omitted in the 1960 edition published by ourselves, and has been omitted here. As have been most parts of the "blurbs" on and in the jacket of the Regnery hardbound copies. But otherwise the whole original content of both treatises has been reprinted without change or omissions, even as to the footnotes which were added in 1960. And we hope that these impassioned reviews of the steps in our earlier betrayal of Chiang and of China, written while the events were still current or recent news, will prove helpful to many patriotic Americans as some trustworthy background to the still further betrayal by our government that is in process at the present time. R.W.

MAY GOD FORGIVE US!

The Letter Begins

Dear Mr. — :

Your letter of May 8 was read with careful interest. The delay in this reply was made necessary by a short business trip to South America, two candy conventions and some other business meetings in Chicago, and the pressure of my regular work. For it was clear that only a long letter on my part would serve the need, and not until this holiday have I been able even to begin one.

At first glance it seems strange that two men, of obvious good will and of strong patriotic purpose, should read the signs of the times so differently. The best that I can do, in support of my interpretation of motives and events, is to set forth the facts which lead me to the convictions, expressed in my Portland speech, to which you refer. I am sorry that I cannot do this in a few brief paragraphs. For I have to go far afield, and build up these facts step by step, in order to show the ultimate impact and significance of the partly completed pattern as it now appears to me.

In reality I have to begin ten thousand miles away, and twenty-five years ago. The title of my speech before the New England Council of Young Republicans was *Acheson and MacArthur*. Some of the material I drew upon in that talk has since been batted around, quite ineffectually, in the Senatorial investigation. Much of it has not; for as members of the

House have charged, none of the Senators on the investigating committee either knew, or took the trouble to find out, the right questions to ask. But more important than this failure of the Senators concerned, to steep themselves in the background of the situation they were investigating, has been the failure of anybody with authoritative knowledge to put together the events leading up to that situation in one connected and coherent story. I do not claim to have any such authoritative knowledge, but I shall use such ability as I can muster to integrate into one readable sequence some of the piecemeal history presented by those who do.

It is a disturbing story. Making all due allowance for my lack of skill in assembling these facts, I still do not think you will sleep as well tonight after reading even this amateurish exposition. And it is a terribly important story. I hope that your own serious interest in our whole foreign policy will fortify your patience, to bear with me line by line while I present it as well as I can.

II
THE BACKGROUND IN CHINA

Although Lenin himself believed that China would be the first of the world's great nations, outside of Russia, to be taken over by the Communists in their march to world rule, and the United States of America the last, and although the Communists first began to work in China in 1920, it was not until 1926-27 that the results of their efforts became noticeable. By that time Earl Browder, Michael Borodin, and several other Communists had infiltrated into the Kuomintang as advisers and protégés of Dr. Sun Yat-sen, or of Madame Sun Yat-sen after her husband's death. Earl Browder is well if unfavorably known to American readers. Borodin will be remembered by some as an ex-jewel smuggler and early agent of the Communist International in this country, and by others as the highly important Moscow functionary of twenty years later, who was liaison official between the Soviet Foreign Office and American newspapermen.

Unfortunately for their purposes, Dr. Sun Yat-sen had died in 1925, too early for them to be ready to seize the opportunity thus offered. And although Borodin in particular had played up to General Chiang Kai-shek, the first thing the General did, after consolidating his position as Sun Yat-sen's successor to top power in the Kuomingtang, was to turn against this group of borers from within. So the Communists, with the help of Madame Sun Yat-sen, and while Chiang was on the famous "Northern" campaign in 1927, seized the mechanisms of power at the capital city of Hankow and attempted to constitute themselves a central government. Chiang turned back and drove the whole crowd, by force of arms, in a complete rout out of Hankow. Browder came back to America,[1] and Borodin fled to Russia to edit the *Moscow News.*

This first Communist attempt on China was completely demolished, but some of its reverberations last until today. For Chiang Kai-shek thus became one of the two men, Franco being the other, who has ever beaten the Communists at their own game. There thus began, for reasons that are obvious, the longest and most vicious smear campaign in all history. It is a smear campaign which has colored, for the outside world, a great deal of what Chiang has done or tried to do ever since. And there thus began at the same time that unholy alliance between Madame Sun Yat-sen and the Russian Communists which has been so harmful to China. Living in Moscow, acting as the "goddess" of Sun Yat-sen University in that city, for the training of Chinese students in Communist tactics and guerilla warfare, and appearing publicly with Stalin to welcome Chinese delegations, she has been a traitor to China in fact if not by intention for more than twenty years.

The second Communist attempt on China, the one which

has persisted ever since, was started in 1929 [2] by Joseph Stalin, who had already come to almost supreme power in Russia. It has been conducted from the very first with that combination of cunning, ruthlessness, patience, and twisting with times and events, that is so typical of this dictator. Stalin began by picking a young Chinese intellectual named Mao Tse-tung as his agent; by having this agent undergo a metamorphosis of outward characteristics; and, leaving the cities alone, by planting Mao and his handful of helpers in a rural province of China to promote Communism under the guise of "agrarian reform." It is worth noting here that Mao, trained in Moscow, guided by Moscow, supported at every turn by Moscow, has never been anything but a murderous tool of Stalin, as was well known by most of the traitors and their gullible dupes who promoted the "agrarian reform" myth for American public opinion.

It is worth noting, too, that "agrarian reform" at its very best, as practised by the Communists, means taking all land away from its former owners, then hauling those owners into "peoples' courts" on trumped up charges, and sentencing them "leniently" to having both hands chopped off. Some recent articles in the *Saturday Evening Post* by a physician who had worked behind the Chinese Communist lines were quite factual and revealing. At its worst, "agrarian reform" means to Stalin the deliberate and literal starvation of some three million Ukrainian peasant farmers, and then boasting to Winston Churchill about it fifteen years later, as the only way it was feasible to collectivize the farms into plots big enough for tractors to be used.

The "agrarian reformers" under Mao, in 1929, proceeded from the very first according to blueprint by forming a Chinese Red Army. Mao's right hand man was "General" Chu Teh; his next in civilian command was Chou En-lai. These are the same two men who, next to Mao, are in top command of the Communist armies fighting our boys in Korea today. But

4

down in Kiangsi province in the early 1930's they were not doing so well, and in 1933 Chiang was able to drive them out. Under Chu Teh's generalship Mao's small forces executed the famous "long march" of about a thousand miles,[3] from Kiangsi all the way to the northwest province of Shensi. There they started the same type of "agrarian reform" afresh. And by 1937 they were still just a handful of Russian stooges, spreading terror in a limited area and trying to get ahead.

Then an entirely new factor changed the Mao-Stalin outlook. Japan felt ready, in the march of its confident imperialism, to proceed with the brazen conquest of China, and began its attack on Shanghai on August 13, 1937. The threat to Russia and to Stalin's own ambitions, from a Japan constantly expanding and growing in military might, was very real. What's more, the inevitable confusion that would be caused in China by the invading Japanese forces was exactly what Stalin knew how to use to best advantage. So he ordered his stooge Mao to form a "united front" with Chiang Kai-shek against the Japanese. And on September 22, 1937 the "Communist Party" announced that its former "Red Army" had been reorganized as a part of the Chinese National Army.

Such an official reorganization did theoretically take place, for Chiang was desperate for all the help and all the "Chinese unity," that could possibly be obtained to hold off the Japanese. Most of the Chinese Communist armed forces were constituted as China's 18th Group Army, with about 45,000 men. But it still remained under the command of the same Communist General Chu Teh, as before. A short time later the remaining ten thousand armed Communists were officially designated as China's New Fourth Army, also under the command of a Communist general. For about two years, until it became clear that China was not going to cave in under the Japanese attack, and probably obvious to Stalin that America would presently be in a war with Japan, the Chinese Communist forces did do some fighting against the Japanese, and refrained from too much troublemaking for the Nationalist forces in China. But they never actually merged with the Nationalist armies or submitted to military control by the Nationalist command; and from the first they claimed an autonomy that was inconsistent with any sound military organization, or with their own pledges at the time Chiang had accepted the "united front."

By the middle of 1939 the situation had become so bad that Chiang told Chou En-lai he would no longer tolerate this pretended autonomy. But by this time the Communists were ready to begin a steady expansion of their occupied area at the expense of civil war in China. And in January, 1940, directly disobeying orders from Generalissimo Chiang, the New Fourth Army moved into zones in Anhwei Province in order to begin establishing a Communist corridor from their stronghold in Shensi all the way to the east coast. The government had no other course than to disband the mutinous troops. But instead of telling the world what had happened, and disclosing the conclusive proofs of treason which were found on officers of the captured Fourth Army, the Nationalist Government tried hard to hush the whole thing up. They thought that such evidence of civil strife would be harmful in their relations with other governments. As a consequence the Communists flooded the press of the world with stories about Chiang's unwarranted oppression of his "Communist allies" which were just about as truthful as the usual Communist propaganda.

But this was only the beginning, and far worse was soon to come. From 1940 on Chiang was compelled to immobilize some of his own forces, so badly needed for fighting the Japanese, to keep Mao's Communists from overrunning more and more territory. And in 1942, after America had come into the war, Stalin felt that he had nothing ultimately to fear from Japan on the Asiatic frontier. In helping to persuade America to neglect the Pacific and throw all of its strength into the European struggle, he had two main purposes. One was to save European Russia from Hitler's armies. The other was to keep the war going in China as long as possible, because every day that Japan's defeat there could be delayed was just that much more opportunity for Mao to increase Communist strength in the confusion.

So immediately after Pearl Harbor there was a reaffirmation between Russia and Japan of the Molotov-Matsuoka Pact.[4] This was something which the Russophiles were careful to keep under wraps at the time, and which they have been trying — with remarkable success — to have the world forget about ever since. The most important part of this pact was a five-year pledge on the part of both nations to commit no act of aggression against each other. Here we had been attacked by Japan. Instead of fighting back at our attacker we were rushing over to Europe, with all the military pressure we could exert and all the matériel of war we could possibly send, at whatever expense of lives and money, to protect and save Russia in its desperate plight before Hitler's armies. And this Russia we were trying so hard to save not only calmly confirmed its alliance with our enemy Japan, who had attacked us, but used that alliance as a means of crippling more and more our ally China, which was fighting on our side against this enemy Japan and had already been fighting this same enemy for four years. The cold-blooded cynicism of this deal is only less astounding than Stalin's correct assumption that our government would swallow it — so far had the Stalinites already gone, through propaganda and treason, in influencing our governmental course.

The formal result of this pact was a state of complacent neutrality between Russia and Japan for over three years. Each could proceed about its own nefarious purposes without worrying about being sideswiped by the other. And

7

in actual truth, the only reason this worked out all to the advantage of Russia and to no benefit for Japan was that America happened to be on the side of Russia and against Japan. The chief practical result was the free hand that Stalin thus gave himself and Mao to begin the real dismemberment of China. Mao resumed the civil war in earnest. His forces began infiltrating and seizing area after area in North China. Despite the Molotov-Matsuoka Pact, Mao could still engage in guerilla tactics against the Japanese, because of the fiction that the Russians had no control over the Chinese Communists — just as Russia maintains the *formal* fiction that she has nothing to do with the Korean fighting today. And there was great propaganda value for Mao, as well as a means of getting actual and direct American help, in putting up an appearance of fighting the Japanese. But even his rule-of-thumb instructions to his generals to devote thirty percent of their effort to fighting the Japanese and seventy percent to fighting Chiang finally became valid only in appearance. And of course the increasing quantities of Chiang's forces that had to be used to withstand this armed Communist encroachment far more than offset any damage inflicted on the Japanese by Mao.

For by 1945 Mao's army had grown to over a million men[5]. In 1937 these Communists had controlled territory in Shensi, with a total of less than 500,000 inhabitants, or about 1/8 of 1% of the population of China.[6] By 1945 they controlled large parts of the populous provinces of Hopei, Chahar, Jehol, Shansi, Shantung, Kiangsu and Anhwei. This they had been enabled to do by Japan's attack on China. During the really effective last four years of this time, this man Mao had been fighting against our active ally Chiang, while we were at war. Yet this is the man that the Communist traitors in our midst and their dupes and allies have persuaded us to befriend in every way, at the expense of our ally Chiang, since 1945 — when Chiang Kai-shek and the

Chinese, worn out and impoverished with eight years of fighting Japanese invaders, had earned and so badly needed our help and friendship instead of the betrayal we have given them.

III
STEPS OF BETRAYAL

You may be asking how all of this has sufficient bearing on contemporary American foreign policy and on today's national politics to justify the space I have given it. But I hope you will accept my assurance that it does, and that you will be convinced as to the accuracy of this assurance before my letter is finished. For the word "betrayal" was used deliberately and advisedly above. And the next step in this letter, to see how this betrayal was stage-managed, brings us much closer home.

For in 1945, when we and our ally China had won the war with the Japanese — and China was our only really effective ally in that war — it would have seemed utterly inconceivable that Mao's Communists could conquer the country within five years. And certainly it was impossible by force. But it was accomplished nevertheless, by an almost unbelievable combination of trickery, chicanery, and treason. At every step Mao could have been stopped by our government, and usually by simply carrying out orders of the American Congress and giving Chiang the supplies Congress had actually voted him. Instead we deliberately turned over rule of China's four hundred million people to Stalin's stooge. Let's look at some of the steps and forces which brought this about.

1. The first was allowing Russia to seize Manchuria. At Yalta, in January and February of 1945, Alger Hiss helped to arrange to give Stalin Port Arthur, Dairen, the Kurile Islands, and Outer Mongolia. Chiang Kai-shek and our Chinese allies were neither present, nor consulted, nor even advised of this

9

monstrous deal. The gift was supposed to be a bribe to get Russia to enter the war. The bribe was put through despite the expressed knowledge of our military commanders that the Japs were collapsing and Russian help was not needed, and despite a specific and urgent message from MacArthur to President Roosevelt pleading against letting Russia come in at all.

For it was obvious then to any honest and informed observer that Russia wanted to enter the war in Japan at the last minute, for the prestige, the booty grabbing, and the place at subsequent council tables which she would claim as one of the victors. The disgraceful folly of the course we had pursued in Europe, in stopping our armies to allow Russia to become the *de facto* conqueror of Berlin and Prague and Vienna, was already perfectly evident to any military man with patriotism and common sense. MacArthur was bitterly opposed to repeating this idiocy – or treason – with the likelihood of even more disastrous results, in the Far East.

Nevertheless the huge concession of somebody else's territory and peoples was made. Russia then kept the war going as long as she possibly could, even by having Malik conceal for two months the first Japanese attempts at surrender – the same Malik who has been screaming his head off at the United Nations over the past many months. When the Japanese Emperor finally succeeded in reaching American commanders with an offer to surrender, despite this duplicity of what they thought was a friendly "neutral" embassy, Russia declared war on Japan just six days before the surrender became effective.

But the arrangements which had been made under this pretense of buying Russia as our ally were a great deal more far-reaching than the mere handout of certain specified booty. For they practically invited Russia to march in and take over Manchuria. This she proceeded to do – with well over a billion dollars worth of American arms and supplies that had been furnished her Far East army in 1944 and 1945!

It is worth pausing a minute over that fact. In 1944 and 1945 Russia not only was not our ally in that part of the world, she was the ally of our enemy Japan. There was no military or political justification for our sending to her Far East army one gun or one shell, especially when all of our production of munitions was still so badly needed by both our allies and ourselves. Yet during that time somebody in our State Department found means and excuses to send these trans-Siberian forces of Stalin, nevertheless, more than twice as much war matériel as we sent to Chiang Kai-shek during the whole four years of his desperate fighting as our ally. And whereas all help that we sent to Stalin, and to every one of our European allies, was turned over to their governments outright, that provided for Chiang was dribbled out to him under the most humiliating terms by our agents in China.

But the main point of this section is that, using our arms and supplies, Stalin's army did grab all of Manchuria, loot it of approximately two billion dollars' worth of industrial equipment, and then turn the province over to Mao as a base of operations. It is from their sanctuaries within Manchuria that Mao has flown his Russian-made jets and marched his protected armies, to inflict sixty-five thousand casualties on our American boys and to devastate completely the whole peninsula of Korea.

2. The second necessary step was for the United States to be persuaded, by the traitors and their dupes and allies within our government, to pull all of our forces out of China, so that Mao could have a free hand. This was easily accomplished.

3. The third step was the persuasion of the United States to supply no arms to Chiang. When the war ended in 1945 there were in India huge stockpiles of war matériel which, under pressure of our military leaders that could not be evaded, had got that far on their way to Chiang. These

supplies were actually *destroyed.* Then in March of 1946 General George C. Marshall, perennial "good soldier" of the State Department, clamped a ten-months embargo on even the sale of arms and replacements to Nationalist China, at the very time that Russia was giving Mao all of the immense Japanese army reserves of war matériel that had been stockpiled in Manchuria.

(Incidentally, within the three months immediately preceding the date of this letter, the Communist steamer *Ming Shan* has taken steel and machinery and a thousand tons of rubber from Hong Kong to Mao's forces. A Danish freighter, the *Heinrich Jessen*, has taken a shipload of steel into Tientsin. The Soviet ship *Vilnus* has carried into Asiatic Soviet ports, from Singapore, one load of six thousand tons of rubber. And our naval ships, *under orders from our State Department,* have been compelled to stand by and allow these supplies to be delivered to our enemies, right under their noses, and while such supplies were being used daily to enable Mao's armies to kill our sons and brothers only a few hundred miles away.)

4. As a fourth step the United States was persuaded to take a position of formal neutrality between the recognized, friendly, and established government of China, and the Communist terrorists. In practice the insistence of U.S. representatives, and especially of General George Marshall, that the "rights" and aspirations and claims of the Communists be given equal consideration with those of the Nationalist Government itself had the net effect of immensely helping Mao. And this policy was deliberately persisted in despite overwhelming proof that the Mao Communists sought the disruption rather than the unity of China, and would break every agreement and every article of faith just as fast as they were agreed upon, no matter how favorable a concession on the part of the Chiang government, to the Communists, they may have seemed at the time.

Here are some extracts from General Marshall's own report of January 7, 1947, on his mission to China:

The dyed-in-the-wool Communists do not hesitate at the most drastic measures to gain their end as, for instance, the destruction of communications in order to wreck the economy of China and produce a situation that would facilitate the overthrow or collapse of the Government, without any regard to the immediate suffering of the people involved. . . .

However, a very harmful and immensely provocative phase of the Chinese Communist Party procedure has been in the character of its propaganda. I wish to state to the American people that in the deliberate misrepresentation and abuse of the action, policies and purposes of our Government this propaganda has been without regard for the truth, without any regard whatsoever for the facts, and has given plain evidence of a determined purpose to mislead the Chinese people and the world and to arouse a bitter hatred of Americans. . . .

Incidentally, the Communist statements regarding the Anping incident which resulted in the death of three Marines and the wounding of twelve others were almost pure fabrication, ...

Most certainly, the course which the Chinese Communist Party has pursued in recent months indicated an unwillingness to make a fair compromise. It has been impossible to get them to sit down at a conference table with government representatives to discuss given issues. Now the Communists have broken off negotiations by their last offer, which demanded the dissolution of the National Assembly and a return to the military positions of January 13, which the Government could not be expected to accept. . . .

The Communists by their unwillingness to compromise in the national interest are evidently counting on an economic collapse to bring about the fall of the Government, accelerated by an extensive guerilla action against the long lines of rail communications — regardless of the cost in suffering to the Chinese people. . . .

The salvation of the situation, as I see it, would be the assumption of leadership by the liberals in the Government and in the minority parties, a splendid group of men, but who as yet lack the political power to exercise a controlling influence. Successful action on their part under the leadership of General-

13

issimo Chiang Kai-shek would, I believe, lead to unity through good government.

In fact, the National Assembly has adopted a democratic constitution which in all major respects is in accordance with the principles laid down by the all-party Political Consultative Conference of last January. It is unfortunate that the Communists did not see fit to participate in the Assembly since the constitution that has been adopted seems to include every major point that they wanted.

Necessarily, I have taken some of these quotations out of context. The statement also contains criticisms of the Kuomingtang, of course. In discussing the Communists' "wholesale disregard of facts" Marshall adds: "In the interest of fairness, I must state that the Nationalist Government publicity agency has made numerous misrepresentations, though not of the vicious nature of the Communist propaganda."

But his chief complaint against the Kuomingtang was that "reactionaries" among them refused to believe that the Communists had any real intention other than the destruction and conquest of China, or to take any of the promises or agreements of the Communists in good faith, or to believe that honest cooperation by the Chinese Communist Party in the Government was conceivable. Nevertheless, in accordance with his instructions from President Truman and Dean Acheson, Marshall kept insisting rigidly on such cooperation, and acceptance of the Communists into the Government, as a prerequisite to help from our government, or even decent treatment on the part of our government, in the economic situation being made constantly more desperate by the tactics of those very Communists.

The net result of this "neutrality" meddling, on the part of a supposed friend holding out promises of great help so badly needed, was disastrous. For it is clear now that in the period from December, 1945 to December, 1946, China still had

14

sufficient remaining strength, and Chiang's armies were still strong enough in comparison with those of Mao — after all, Chiang's armies had held at bay nearly three million[7] Japanese in China, most of whom would otherwise have been fighting us — to have crushed the Communists entirely. The demand of the Communists in December, 1946, that military positions be restored to those of the preceding January, is unwitting evidence quoted by Marshall himself as to what had happened militarily during the year despite everything. But it was exactly during this period of December, 1945, to December, 1946, that General Marshall forced on Chiang Kai-shek three separate truces with the Communists, giving them a chance each time to stave off defeat and regroup their forces. In the light of these developments it is pathetic to hear Marshall complaining in January, 1947 — in this same report — about "the irreconcilable Communists who, I must state, did not so appear last February."

There was sad irony in this situation for Chiang, as well as frustration and the makings of despair. He knew that every suggestion of peaceful unity on the part of the Communists was merely pretense, that their every apparent concession to civilized procedures was merely an act of going through motions, and that any compromise arrangement, no matter how solemnly agreed to, was to them only a stepping stone from which to move on again as soon as expedient; and that they had no real interest whatsoever in any "solution" except their ultimate conquest of all China. He had known Mao and his chief lieutenants, their tactics and purposes, well, and he had been fighting them, for twenty years. He had put them down successfully and repeatedly until the long and crushing Japanese invasion and then the weight of Russia's assistance had given Mao his chance. But here he was being told, month after month and actually year after year, by representatives of the one great ally on whom he should have been able to depend for help, that anybody in his own government who

15

could not believe the Chinese Communists to be "agrarian reformers," and idealists at heart, was a reactionary who had to be tossed out of his government; and that this government had to be "broadened" by taking the Communists in. Since the Communists themselves made sure that the latter demand could never be fulfilled, the result reached all the way to an embargo on our sale of arms to Chiang with which to fight these Communists. And in President Truman's own published statement of December 18, 1946, in which he reports that in August China had purchased — not been given — all of our surplus property that was rotting in the Pacific areas ("rapid deterioration of the material in open storage under tropical conditions" was the phrase used), he boasted that aircraft and non-demilitarized combat material had been excluded; and that "thus, no weapons which could be used in fighting a civil war were made available through this agreement."

Until December, 1941, Japan had conducted its four-years' invasion of China under specious terminologies that avoided a formal declaration of war. Immediately after Japan attacked us at Pearl Harbor, Chiang Kai-shek's government declared war on Japan, on Germany, and on Italy. His simple message to President Roosevelt read as follows: "To our new common battle we offer all we are and all we have, to stand with you until the Pacific and the world are freed from the curse of brute force and endless perfidy."

Not all of the twenty-five years of vicious smearing by the Communists and their sympathizers, nor the half-baked criticisms of his government by those who know nothing of China's problems have ever been able to make of Chiang Kai-shek personally anything but a Christian gentleman. He lived up to that pledge with the "all we had," and undoubtedly saved tens of thousands of American lives by doing so. Never has an ally deserved better of a companion nation in · arms. Never has one been let down, instead, more completely, more ignobly, nor with more of that

16

very perfidy which was to have been abolished by the fight.

5. A fifth important step, so necessary to the purposes of the Communist sympathizers, was the suppression of the Wedemeyer report. The report was dated September 19, 1947. That General Marshall wrote a letter to President Truman concerning the report, in which he said "I think this should be suppressed," and that President Truman wrote in his own hand on the margin of this letter "I agree – H.T.", and that the report was completely suppressed until far too late for it to do Chiang any good, is all well-known history now.

The accurate presentation in that report of Soviet aims and purposes was more than sympathizers with those purposes, or their dupes and allies, could allow to appear. And just one of Wedemeyer's major suggestions, that Manchuria be put under a United Nations trusteeship, could certainly have prevented the Korean war and sixty-five thousand American casualties. For his honesty and unshakable patriotism Wedemeyer was taken out of circulation by assignment to a minor post, and has since been led by the futility of his position to resign from the army – our youngest and probably ablest Lieutenant General, sacrificed to the pro-Soviet pressure group, and as a warning to anybody else, in government or out, who dares stand up and throw facts in their face.

6. The sixth of the important and necessary chronological steps was, when the tide had completely turned and all China was falling to the Communists too obviously for denial, to persuade the United States still to take no stand and no step which would prevent the catastrophe. Even Mao must have been unable to believe his good luck. Time after time, by a firm United States stand, Mao would have been stopped in his tracks and afraid to go further. Instead of taking such a stand, our government rebuffed Chiang at every turn and every appeal. And until recent developments made such a

position politically untenable, at least temporarily, this policy of throwing Chiang overboard was to have been continued until even Formosa was in Communist hands. But that is getting a little ahead of my story.

IV
HISS AND COMPANY

For it is time now to start looking at the American section of this picture. In the pages above I have spoken of this or that end having been accomplished by the traitors and their dupes and allies in our government. It is time to show how these traitors and their dupes and allies have accomplished such ends; by infiltrating and controlling organizations already extant; by setting up numberless deceptive new ones; and by achieving an amazing domination of our State Department, both as individuals and through these organizations.

There is no chance to look at all, or even at an appreciable fraction, of these fronts, organizations, and developments. We shall have to pick as samples just a few of those which are both important and pertinent to our present topic of discussion.

1. The most important of all organizations within that category, without doubt, is the famous Institute of Pacific Relations. It was founded, and financed by American philanthropy of the "Carnegie" type, as a supposedly unbiased fact-finding and educational agency to promote international peace, understanding, and friendly relations in the Pacific area of the world. It had acquired great prestige, and become a terrifically important medium for influencing public opinion. And during the 1930's this organization was gradually infiltrated and practically taken over by the Communists, their dupes and their allies.

Administration of the IPR was in the hands of an Executive Committee of eight, plus a Chairman and a

Secretary, chosen from and by the trustees. Among the trustees, during the 1940's, were Henry Wallace, Alger Hiss, F. Mortimer Graves, Len DeCaux, Donald G. Tewkesbury, Lauchlin Currie, and Maxwell S. Stewart.

Wallace you know about. Also Alger Hiss. F. Mortimer Graves had been Chairman of the Washington Committee for Aid to China, officially cited by government agencies as a Communist Front. Graves promoted a Paul Robeson concert in Washington in 1941, and a check-up revealed that the proceeds of that concert had gone to a Communist party organization. (Remember Graves was the *promoter* of the affair.)

Lauchlin Currie was later named by Elizabeth Bentley as one of her top Washington contacts, when she was a Russian spy, in securing information to send to Russia. Currie was also named as a Communist fellow-worker by Whittaker Chambers.

Maxwell Stewart was a former teacher at the Moscow Institute, and his name has appeared on fifty-two different organizations cited by government agencies as subversive.

These were among the trustees. Four of the actual members of the Executive Committee of ten were Edward C. Carter, Secretary General, Owen Lattimore, Frederick Vanderbilt Field, and Harriet Lucy Moore. We'll take time for only some sample indications of where their loyalties or sympathies lay.

Edward C. Carter had received from Stalin himself the *Order of the Red Banner of Labor*. In 1938 he had signed a statement defending the notorious and infamous Moscow purge trials.

Owen Lattimore had also been on the editorial board of *Amerasia,* of which more presently. He resigned from the board in 1941, and gives the noblest reasons for having joined in the first place. As early as 1937 Mr. Lattimore, along with Philip J. Jaffe and T.A. Bisson, paid a visit to the Chinese

19

Communists at Yenan. There is a picture extant of these three posing in Yenan and a letter extant from Agnes Smedley telling Jaffe how grateful she and her fellow Communists were "to all of you. There has never been anything like this here before." Though Mr. Lattimore claims to have had "no connection with *Amerasia* after 1941," he admits that on the Sunday three days prior to the arrests in that case, both Andrew Roth and John Service were at his house, getting his advice on the galley proofs of Roth's forthcoming book. Service and Roth were among the six *Amerasia* leaders arrested by the F.B.I. three days later. Mr. Lattimore fails to mention some matters concerning two such good friends, which and who will turn up later in this letter. But Mr. Lattimore, for most excellent reasons in connection with his writings, goes out of his way to condemn "guilt by omission." Mr. Lattimore is a very smart man. I defy anybody, unless extremely well-informed as to background, to read just twenty pages of any of his books and not decide that here is an honest idealist; misguided or prejudiced, perhaps, but an honest idealist nevertheless. But I also defy anybody, who does have any knowledge of the background whatsoever, to read all of *Solution In Asia* and *Ordeal By Slander*, and not come out with the same conviction as my own. Here is the slickest, trickiest, cleverest intellectual eel I have run across in forty years of voracious reading.

Frederick Vanderbilt Field, a columnist for *The Daily Worker*, has long been known as "the millionaire Communist." During this past year he has refused to tell a Congressional Committee whether or not he was a Communist, on the grounds that it might incriminate him.

Harriet Lucy Moore was a contributor to *Amerasia*, and tied in with many other Communist enterprises.[8]

Typical of the publicity methods employed by the IPR under this kind of control was an article published in 1943 in *Far Eastern Survey*, the Institute's official publication. This article, supposed to be an objective analysis of the China situation, was really a poisonous attack on the Chinese Nationalist Government and a eulogy of the Chinese Communists. "There are two Chinas," it said. "One is now generally called Kuomingtang China; the other is called Communist China. However, these are only party labels. To be more descriptive the one might be called feudal China, the other democratic China."

Please remember that this was in *1943,* when the Chinese Nationalist Government was holding back three million Japanese on Chinese soil.[9] (In case you doubt this number, it is from the official figure of our government in connection with the Japanese armed forces, administrators, technicians, and so forth, that had to be repatriated from China to Japan after V-J day. From President Truman's statement of December 18, 1946, for instance: "There were about 3,000,000 Japanese, nearly one-half of them Army or Navy personnel, to be evacuated." The number officially given in the same report as actually evacuated by November, 1946, was 2,986,438.) The Chinese Communists at that time were a still small but noisy and troublesome bunch of terrorists in the northwest provinces, only making any headway at all because of their ability to take advantage of the load which Chiang and the government of China were carrying as our allies in the fight against Japan.

The whole article was a composite of plain vicious lies, by one T.A. Bisson. Bisson was part of a Communist front called "Friends of the Chinese People," which has been listed by the Attorney General of the U.S. as subversive. Bisson had been a speaker, along with Earl Browder and Philip Jaffe, at dinners given by these "Friends" in 1934 and 1935. He was later a member of the editorial board of *Amerasia.* He was one of the notorious four hundred who followed every turn of the Stalinist line so closely as to have *endorsed* the Hitler-Stalin pact that set off World War II.

21

This was the kind of "impartial" authority given wide publication by the Institute of Pacific Relations. But the IPR had much more direct and important influence in other ways. As Benjamin Gitlow says, through the IPR the Communists bored their way into our State Department. It had amazing success in placing its chosen agents in high positions in American agencies dealing with China. It was a virtual employment agency, managed by Carter and Graves, for pro-Communist personnel.

In the notes for my speech that started all of this I have ten illustrations of such Communists or Communist sympathizers who were placed in positions of great importance in our State Department by the IPR. But it requires too much space to document the Communist sympathies of even this fraction of the total number placed, for one thing. And for another, because there is always the chance of doing some individual an injustice through a mistaken interpretation of his actions, I have no desire to name names except where they seem essential to the thread and the convincingness of the story. There already are and will have to be too many actual names in this letter for me to be happy about the necessity for such identifications. But whereas a mistake is always possible with regard to some one individual here and there, there is no such possibility of a mistaken interpretation of the sympathies, purposes, and results achieved by such groups as a whole as that which has long controlled the Institute of Pacific Relations.

2. Since we have mentioned *Amerasia* so often, let's look next at that publication and the group behind it. Early in 1945, the F.B.I. learned that somebody in the State Department was feeding this magazine confidential reports and papers. After several months of careful investigation, on June 6, 1945 the F.B.I. arrested Kate L. Mitchell, Editor; Philip J. Jaffe, Co-Editor; Mark J. Gayn, contributor; John S. Service, State Department Foreign Service Officer; Em-

manuel S. Larsen, State Department Research Expert on China Affairs; and Andrew Roth, Liaison Officer between Naval Intelligence and the State Department. In the *Amerasia* offices in New York were found more than one hundred files of top-secret documents stolen from the State Department, War Department, Navy Department, Office of Strategic Services, and Office of War Information. Among these papers was a detailed report showing the disposition of every unit in Chiang Kai-shek's army!

Immediately, some very high mysterious influence went to work to hush up the case. The Department of Justice representatives presented it to the Grand Jury in such a way that only Jaffe, Larsen, and Roth were indicted. Since you will be hearing more about John S. Service, it is particularly worth noting that Acheson's influence was definitely exerted on his behalf, and his case was dropped; despite the fact that the F.B.I. showed, among other things, that a Russian agent, Max Granich, had acted as go-between for Jaffe and Service. (And despite the fact that Service had just recently been fired by Pat Hurley from our embassy in Chungking, and sent back to America because of his pro-Communist activities.) Mark J. Gayn was cleared despite the fact that two hundred secret documents were found in his apartment. Later the case against Roth was nol-prossed. Jaffe was allowed to plead guilty, and fined $2,500.00. Larsen was fined $500.00. That was all. Neither heaven nor earth has been able to open the case since, despite several congressional attempts. This was treason, nothing else; plain unqualified, indefensible treason. But the perpetrators could not be reached. The traitors, their dupes, and allies were already too strongly entrenched.

3. For a sample of some of the activities of the traitors, their dupes, and allies, working as individuals instead of through organizational fronts, one good place to take a look is at the American Embassy in Chungking under Major General Patrick Hurley. He was appointed a special envoy to

China on August 18, 1944, and given the full rank of Ambassador on November 30. He remained in China until September, 1945.[10]

The fact that Hurley succeeded Henry Wallace and preceded George Marshall in their missions to China is a pretty good indication of the outlook the State Department assumed him to have when they gave him the job. He was definitely thought in many quarters to be pro-Mao, and there is little doubt as to his having swallowed enough pro-Mao propaganda to be biased in that direction. He was sent to persuade Chiang to take the Communists into a coalition government, and he set out to accomplish that purpose.

But Hurley had a mind of his own, and was honest. In time he was completely disillusioned. When he began really to open his eyes he was amazed. He found that the embassy was loaded with Communist sympathizers and active pro-Communist workers. He found, among other things, that some of these officials were not only sending secret reports to Washington, contradicting his recommendations, but that copies of these reports were also going directly to the Chinese Communists. Finally Hurley fired summarily, and sent home from Chungking, eleven American embassy officials who were, in his opinion, too pro-Communist to be of any use in China. Hurley himself returned to Washington, to have a showdown. He had one, got what he thought were reasonable instructions, and then — I know this sounds like something out of an Oppenheim novel, but it is historical fact, nevertheless — was double-crossed by having those instructions actually changed in the course of the stenographic copying during the night. He immediately resigned, with a blast which included the following:

"The professional foreign service men sided with the Communist armed party and the imperialistic bloc of nations whose policy it was to keep China divided against herself. Our professional diplomats continuously advised the Commu-

24

nists that my efforts in preventing the collapse of the National Government did not represent the policy of the United States. These same professionals openly advised the Communist armed party to decline unification of the Chinese Communist Army with the National Army unless the Communists were given control." Hurley demanded an investigation, but mysterious influences again prevented it. The Communist traitors, their dupes, and allies were too strongly entrenched, especially in the State Department.

Now, as the most important part of this whole episode, consider this. Among the eleven men fired by Hurley and sent home from Chungking, as too pro-Communist to be any good, were these:

George Atcheson Jr.	Edward E. Rice
John P. Davies Jr.	Arthur Ringwalt
Fulton Freeman	John S. Service
Hungerford B. Howard	Philip D. Sprouse
Raymond P. Ludden	

And every single one of these men was then actually promoted by our State Department.

John P. Davies became a member, representing the Far East, in the Top Planning Board, which drafts overall State Department policy. Ringwalt was appointed Chief of the China Division of the State Department. Rice and Freeman became Assistant Chiefs of the China Division. Both Ludden and Howard were sent back to China in the American consular service. And John S. Service and George Atcheson were actually sent to Japan to advise MacArthur.

MacArthur flatly refused to have Service, so he was brought back home and — after Dean Acheson succeeded George Marshall as Secretary of State — was put in charge of placements and promotions in the Department. This man who had been arrested by the F.B.I. for treasonous activities, a man with a long record of pro-Communist sympathies and actions, was put by Acheson in position to determine who should do what work, and who promoted and who not, in the State Department.

4. Let's look at just a very few more illustrations along these lines, before proceeding at long last to the body and main theme of this letter.

From 1937 to 1943 the Chief of the Far Eastern Office in our State Department was one Maxwell M. Hamilton, a friend of Alger Hiss who was named along with Hiss on that list of eleven hundred Communist fellow-travelers on the Federal payroll cited in 1941 by the House Un-American Activities Committee.

In 1944 John Carter Vincent became Director of China Affairs, and in 1945 Director of the Office of Far Eastern Affairs. He threw the weight of his office in every way he could in favor of Mao and against Chiang. One illustration of his outlook towards the whole Asiatic picture will have to suffice. General MacArthur, at a critical point in his effort to keep Russia out of a vetoing role in Japan, issued a warning against the threat of Communism in the island. In September, 1946, Vincent rushed into print to rebuke MacArthur, and to state that MacArthur was violating State Department directives for Japan. These directives, Vincent said, sought to use Japan for "building a bridge of friendship to the Soviet Union."

A whole year before that, or in September, 1945, our Embassy in Moscow had already warned our State Department against putting any confidence in Russia observing either the spirit or the letter of any of its treaties and agreements in the Far East. The Soviet policy since then, especially in support of the Chinese Communists, in direct violation of the treaty it had signed with Nationalist China on August 14, 1945, and in all of its other actions, had clearly shown its intention to spread terror and confusion over all of

Eastern Asia as rapidly as it could. Yet here was our Director of the Office of Far Eastern Affairs willing to toss Japan to the Communists as a means of "building a bridge of friendship with the Soviet Union." Fortunately here was just one more place, and an early one, where MacArthur paid as little attention as he could to either the idiotic or the treasonous directions that he received from Washington.

It is very hard to pin any specific overt Communist connection on Vincent, except by the overwhelming evidence of association. But there has been unearthed one warning, made in 1945 by an official of the Office of Strategic Services, that because of Vincent's association with incidents and individuals involved in leaks of information through the Soviet Embassy to Moscow, no secret information should be divulged that might reach Vincent. He may have been completely innocent of anything but prejudice and stupidity. If so, the help his stupidity gave to the Mao Communists didn't hurt him any, for he was promoted in 1947 to become United States Minister to Switzerland, and remained in that position for about three years. More recently he has been demoted to a consular job in Tangiers, whether because too much heat was finally being turned on for the State Department to keep him so conspicuously exposed, or for some other purpose, I have no idea.

Through all these years and activities two notorious names pop up everywhere. One is that of Owen Lattimore. I have already commented on him just a little and will add only one more incident in this connection. When we had withdrawn our troops from Korea and invitingly abandoned it to possible attack, the question could not be quite ignored, on the surface anyway, as to what should be done if it were attacked. Mr. Acheson turned to Owen Lattimore for advice on this point. And in a secret memorandum to the State Department Lattimore proposed that Korea should be allowed "to fall without making it look as if the United

States had pushed it." I wonder how the mothers of American boys who have been killed in Korea like that as a policy of the American government.

The other name was that of Alger Hiss. Not only was Hiss with the dying Roosevelt at Yalta, whispering advice in his ear, but he was one of four State Department "experts" who had been sent ahead to prepare the notes and directives for the conference. He had become Assistant to the Director of Far Eastern Affairs as early as 1938. He climbed steadily in influence over Far Eastern Affairs, and many of the documents stolen by Hiss which were finally presented by Whittaker Chambers were confidential papers of the Far Eastern Office. At Yalta he was able to give an open road to Manchuria, to Russia, and to lay the groundwork for giving it all of China.

On one of the earlier occasions when the loyalty of Alger and Donald Hiss had been questioned, it was Acheson who had stated that he would vouch for both absolutely, and who had thus shut off the investigation. Even after Hiss was convicted Acheson stated publicly that he would not turn his back on Alger Hiss — he certainly hasn't turned his back on Alger Hiss's policies — and Donald Hiss is still in Acheson's law firm today.

Now there are dozens and dozens more of individuals like those I have mentioned, who had made and carried out our disastrous policies with regard to the Chinese Communists. Almost without exception they have been friends of Acheson, used by him, supported by him, and kept in the State Department by him. And this background is absolutely necessary to a real understanding of the events of the past few weeks. So let's now look at Dean Acheson himself; and largely — but not exclusively — at his acts and policies which have a bearing on MacArthur's role.

V
DEAN ACHESON

A little of some other history is again needed for background. It is to be noted first that Dean Acheson's sympathy for Communist ambitions has not been restricted to those ambitions in the Far East. When still Undersecretary of State, Mr. Acheson forced through a loan of ninety million dollars to the Soviet-controlled Warsaw government of Poland. The loan had been negotiated by Donald Hiss, Alger Hiss's brother, a member of Acheson's law firm. Our Ambassador to Poland, Arthur Bliss Lane, pointing out the Red terror in Poland, the arrests of American citizens and the crushing of all freedoms, appealed to the State Department to refuse the loan. He said: "With the greatest earnestness of which I am capable, I beg the department not to approve the extension of any credits at this time." The loan was approved, nevertheless, and the money was used to strengthen Soviet control of Poland. It was probably this experience which, when a year or two later Acheson was made Secretary of State, prompted Lane to blurt out: "God help the United States!"

In November, 1945, there was a Madison Square Garden rally called by the National Conference of Soviet American Friendship. Its excuse was the welcoming of that extremely pro-Soviet screwball, the red Dean of Canterbury. The speakers included Corliss Lamont, Paul Robeson, and Dean Acheson. Mr. Acheson told the assembled audience of Communists and fellow travelers that there was no specific reason to suppose that the vital interests of the American and Russian people would ever clash. "We understand," he said, "and agree with them to have friendly governments along her borders is essential, both for the security of the Soviet Union and for the peace of the world."

This meant clearly that, so far as Acheson could control the situation, the United States would not oppose Stalin's setting up "friendly governments," which is of course a euphemism for satellite governments, along the Soviet borders. And the State Department under Acheson's domination has acquiesced in the establishment of such satellites in Europe.

It is no wonder that Acheson was early praised by the *Daily Worker*, official organ of the Communist Party, "as one of the most forward looking men in the State Department." And it is interesting to note that in March, 1946, a few months after this Madison Square Garden rally, when Winston Churchill made his speech in Fulton, Missouri, warning the world against real Soviet purposes, and the speech was so bitterly assailed by Moscow and by Communists everywhere, Mr. Acheson snubbed Churchill by refusing to appear at the New York dinner in his honor.

Another item worth including in this brief list is the report on atomic energy, dated March, 1946, which was prepared by Dean Acheson and David Lilienthal together. It proposed giving the secrets of atomic energy, including the bomb, to Russia outright. It stated, "there can be no international cooperation which does not presuppose international community of knowledge." Fortunately, there were some wiser heads which did prevail against this extreme folly. Russia was offered the atomic secrets subject to a continuing inspection, free of the veto, in all countries of their use; and this Russia refused. As we know now, she was getting the atomic secrets by treason anyway.

Then all-important has been Mr. Acheson's coddling and support of subversives in his department. The record is almost unbelievable. Despite continuous warnings from the F.B.I. and from security officers within the State Department itself — at least one of whom was threatened for being overzealous — the infiltration of doubtful characters into the State Department had gone so far by June, 1947, that a Senate appropriations subcommittee addressed a then secret memorandum to George Marshall, then Secretary of State. This memorandum read in part as follows:

It becomes necessary due to the gravity of the situation to call your attention to a condition that developed and still flourishes in the State Department under the administration of Dean Acheson. It is evident that there is a deliberate, calculated program being carried out not only to protect Communist personnel in high places but to reduce security and intelligence protection to a nullity.

On file in the Department is a copy of a preliminary report of the F.B.I. on Soviet espionage activities in the United States, which involves a large number of State Department employees, some in high official positions . . . . Voluminous files are on hand in the Department proving the connection of the State Department employees and officials with this Soviet espionage ring.

Please note that this memorandum was not written by irresponsible rabble-rousers. It was not written by some one Senator, who might be accused of seeking notoriety and votes. It was not written for public consumption at all. It was a dignified, official, intra-government memorandum, prepared in carefully weighed language by a group of United States Senators who were in a position to know what was going on. Keeping that in mind, will you please reread this sentence: "It is evident that there is a *deliberate, calculated* program being carried out not only to protect Communist personnel in high places but to reduce security and intelligence protection to a nullity." But George Marshall did nothing about this report, of course, and no change in the State Department policy referred to has ever become evident. The traitors, their dupes and allies, were too solidly in control.

We could go on with details along these lines almost indefinitely. It was Acheson who went to bat for John Service when he was arrested in the *Amerasia* case. Despite the fact that Service has since admitted turning over secret documents to Philip Jaffe, a known Soviet agent, he has been consistently promoted by Acheson. It was Acheson who prevented the House Un-American Activities Committee from holding public hearings in the case of Sam Carp, a Bridgeport, Connecticut businessman whose sister is Molotov's wife, and whose business relations with the Soviet Union needed some explaning. It was Acheson who rushed to the defense of Lauchlin Currie, who was named as a fellow traveler by both Elizabeth Bentley and Whittaker Chambers. And Currie still stands high in the graces of the State Department today.

It was Acheson who, as late as the middle of 1947, over bitter congressional opposition, insisted on still sending seventeen million dollars worth of post-war lend-lease supplies direct to Russia. It seems that, according to Mr. Acheson, there was some unfinished commitment which made it our moral obligation to do so. But the fact that the Russians were still holding and using *over six hundred* of our ships, and refusing to return them despite the firmest kind of commitment to do so — this apparently involved no moral lapse whatsoever, in the mind of Mr. Acheson. At any rate today, four years later, the Russians still have 670 of the 672 ships, and are still refusing to return another one.

It was Acheson who permitted Valentin Gubitchev, a convicted Russian spy in this country, to depart peacefully for his homeland, while plenty of Americans were and still are being held in Soviet prisons on phony charges — one being Robert Vogeler who was held fifteen months and then turned loose as a physical wreck after our government had met the blackmail demands put forth as a condition for his release.

The record is enormous. So let's call it off here, and get nearer to the crux of our discussion, which is Acheson's acts and policies as they have directly affected MacArthur's part of the world.

VI
ACHESON AND MACARTHUR

It is to be noted that Acheson has had to overcome many opponents in his climb to power; to the present position where he actually dominates our government, and Mr. Truman eats out of his hand. One of the first was Arthur Bliss Lane, whom we have already mentioned. Mr. Acheson won that fight and retired Mr. Lane with relative ease.

Next might be mentioned Adolph Berle, Jr., who first warned Acheson about the Hiss brothers, way back in 1941, or earlier. Berle is certainly no reactionary; he was always an ardent New Dealer. But in 1944 he found himself pressing for a clean-cut showdown with the Russians, while our position was strongest. He has testified under oath as follows: "The opposite group in the State Department was largely the men — Mr. Acheson's group, of course — with Hiss as a principal assistant in the matter . . . . I got trimmed in that fight and, as a result, went to Brazil and that ended my diplomatic career."

Next was Joseph C. Grew, our former Ambassador to Japan, who in 1945 was Undersecretary of State. Acheson was then Assistant Secretary. Grew was opposed to the continuing appeasement of the Russians, and was much concerned about the *Amerasia* revelations. But Grew had served the government for forty-one years, had long passed the age of retirement, was facing the possibility of a major operation, and felt that now the war was over he should be allowed to resign. His insistence on resignation precipitated a savage contest for control in the department. Acheson had Truman's ear, won out, and was made Undersecretary of State in Grew's place. This caused the expected joy in all Communist quarters.[11] The *Daily Worker* publicly exulted, and so did P.M. Talk of any follow-up of the *Amerasia* case was immediately stopped. James C. Dunn, another realist about Russia, was got out of the Department by being made

Ambassador to Italy, and several other opponents of Acheson, including some real authorities on the Far East, were retired.

Other and later casualties to the policies and the rising power of Acheson were Major General Patrick Hurley; Lt. General Wedemeyer; James V. Forrestal, who was literally hounded to his death by sinister forces he could not stop; and Louis Johnson. But the greatest enemy of all, the one it took Acheson longest to move out of his way, was General Douglas MacArthur. From his earliest days in the Department of State, Acheson has done everything he could to belittle, hamstring, and discredit the General. And whatever the significance may be, in this course he has followed, and been supported by, the exact Communist line.

From the very beginning Acheson's policies have been based on the contention that Mao and the Chinese Communists were mere agrarian reformers. MacArthur knew better, and has fought that position. Acheson has claimed that the Chiang Kai-shek regime was too riddled with corruption to be supported. (It's an even bet that, entirely aside from the rampant treason, the corruption in Washington has been far worse, but this does not seem to have disturbed Mr. Acheson any.) MacArthur has made no secret of his friendship for Chiang. And despite the years of smear and of deliberate help in the gradual destruction of Chiang by so many pro-Communist forces, Dr. Hu Shih, one-time Chinese Ambassador to the United States and generally recognized as China's greatest scholar, said in 1949 that "Communism is so implacable and intolerant, so diabolically thorough in its indoctrination and so ruthless in enforcing its totalitarian control even in China that Chiang Kai-shek should be supported despite his shortcomings because he alone sees this and has been uncompromising in resisting it . . ."

Acheson has moved heaven and earth to support the British position, and have this country follow Britain's

34

lead, in the recognition of Red China. MacArthur has opposed this in every way he could.

Acheson has both openly, and insidiously behind the scenes, done everything he could to disparage MacArthur personally. The General's overwhelming success in Japan, despite Acheson's disparagement and active efforts to sabotage MacArthur's program, have kept this campaign from reaching success until this spring. Because of the policies of Acheson and the Acheson clique we have absolutely no friends left in Asia today except the Japanese, the Filipinos, and — until the current betrayal — the South Koreans. They are or were still our friends largely because of MacArthur, and because he is such a personal hero to them. Now MacArthur has been removed, deliberately in such a way that it must connote disgrace in their eyes. And the Voice of America, operated by Mr. Acheson's State Department, has been bleating away continuously with misrepresentations of the reaction to MacArthur's removal in this country. Whatever the purpose may have been, the efforts to show that the American people were practically unanimous in support of Truman's disgrace of their hero must have been terribly discouraging to our remaining Asiatic friends.

It was shortly after Acheson had succeeded Joseph C. Grew as Undersecretary of State that he really went to work openly on MacArthur. The whole Far East Department of the State Department, inspired by Owen Lattimore and his book, *Solution In Asia*, was bent on having a great social and economic revolution in Japan. These schemes required a tremendous army of occupation. The Russians were supporting this position for all they were worth, and were firing all the dirty ammunition they had at MacArthur. They particularly lambasted the General's statement that Japan was calm enough to be occupied by only 200,000 troops. Acheson issued a bitter reprimand, reminding MacArthur that not he, but the State Department was "determining American policy toward Japan." *P.M.* shouted, "Hats off to Dean Acheson." Acheson explained that he had rebuked General MacArthur because he, Acheson, felt the need for a "liberal" government in Japan — a government in whose administration the Soviet Union would have a part. This deliberate confusion of "liberalism" and "communism" has been a consistent theme of Mr. Acheson's utterances — and of course has been the watchword of most pro-Soviet ballyhoo. But as to these arguments about the Japanese occupation, history has already shown who was right; or right, at least, from the point of view of the welfare of the United States and of the Japanese people.

Similar fights had already been going on. Before the Japanese surrender Joseph Grew, his assistant Eugene Dooman, and Joseph Ballantine, then Director of the Office of Far Eastern Affairs — all of whom had had long experience in Tokyo — felt sure that the Japanese would never surrender unless the position of the Emperor was recognized, and that Japan would be ungovernable if the imperial authority was destroyed. This was brilliant farsightedness, based on sound experience — as history since has clearly indicated. Mr. Acheson opposed these views. And though military events moved so rapidly as to bring a climax before he could prevail, the fight was victorious enough from his point of view to cause the resignations of Dooman and Ballantine. In their stead Acheson immediately brought Owen Lattimore into the fold again, as a member of the Pauley Reparations Commission, and promoted John Carter Vincent to director of the Office of Far Eastern Affairs. Lauchlin Currie, another member of the Acheson team, remained attached to the White House.

This group then continued to advocate measures for the Japanese occupation as proposed in Lattimore's book.

These included abolition of the monarchy, banishment of the imperial family to China, dissolution of Japanese business enterprises, a purge of business executives; and taking securities representing ownership of businesses away from their current owners and managers, at a purely nominal price, and selling these securities to farmers' cooperatives and labor unions, many of which were Communist-controlled. MacArthur has shown by every action and every word how much he was opposed to these extreme socialistic and communistic measures; but it was James Forrestal who finally forced a formal reversal of this program, with regard to the Japanese domestic economy, before the pressure of such forces from so many sides caused his death.

It was Acheson and John Carter Vincent who wrote the instructions and the President's statement which was George Marshall's guide for his disastrous year in China. MacArthur made clear his disagreement with such appeasement policies.

Although our War Department well knew, from its own intelligence reports, the actual nature and purposes of the Chinese Communists, and made their G-2 intelligence reports available to the State Department, Acheson's clique overruled and ignored them. And Acheson has constantly denounced Chiang for refusing to take these Communists into his government. MacArthur has made clear his understanding of the folly of taking Communists into any government — as shown by what happened in Poland, Hungary, Rumania, Bulgaria, and Czecho-Slovakia — by refusing to let them into the Japanese government at any point.

Finally, when Chiang's government was at last cracking up, due to our desertion and our support of Mao, and was making its final desperate bid for *some* help, instead of giving help Mr. Acheson's State Department released, on August 5, 1949 its notorious and infamous "White Paper" on China.

Chosen to edit this whitewash of the State Department's ruinous policies towards China over the past several years was Philip C. Jessup. Dr. Jessup was a close friend of Frederick Vanderbilt Field. (Mr. Field, incidentally, has been getting himself into the news rather industriously since my letter was started — including going to jail for refusing to tell who provided the actual bail which he had posted for his four convicted Communist friends now being hunted by the F.B.I.) Dr. Jessup had been closely identified with Field and others of the IPR clique during that campaign against the Chinese Republic. Dr. Jessup had been listed as a sponsor of several Communist fronts. He was a great friend of Alger Hiss, and appeared as a character witness for Hiss at his trial. And of course he was, and is, a protégé of Acheson.

The *New York Times* on the whole has certainly supported and looked favorably on the Administration's foreign policies, which means Mr. Acheson's foreign policies, over the past few years. But the *New York Times* said editorially of the White Paper that "such a summary could not possibly be objective . . . that the State Department certainly would not inform the President that this effort of theirs was misleading, or that its policies had been mistaken . . . that this inquest on China was not the work of a detached coroner but of a vitally interested party in the catastrophe . . . and that at this point one of these vital interests was self-justification."

One of our best informed writers about the Far Eastern situation has said of the White Paper that it is "a masterpiece of omissions, evasions, tricky half-truths, sly slants and twists to create misleading impressions and to conceal grave misjudgments. Its publication marked the lowest point ever reached by American diplomacy."

The whole White Paper was a betrayal of our ally, Chiang Kai-shek, and a defense of that betrayal. There were many terrible things in it. Even the six-thousand-word "summary," which Dean Acheson wrote in the form of a "letter of transmittal" of the White Paper to the President, contains paragraphs which, when considered against the unvarnished historical facts, will literally make you sick in your stomach that an American Secretary of State could put his name to such a document. But probably the worst thing of all about the White Paper was Mr. Acheson's complete before-the-event recognition of the Mao Communists as the conquerors of all mainland China; something which by no means had yet occurred and could still have been prevented. MacArthur during this time was successfully keeping the Communists from getting even any real foothold in Japan.

And for a final "finally," to this part of our discussion, Acheson has schemed and maneuvered in every way that he could to have us abandon Formosa. In a secret memorandum, smoked out by the United Press in January, 1950, the State Department advised its attachés abroad to sell the public the idea that Formosa was of no strategic value. The memorandum stated that politically, geographically, and strategically Formosa was in no way especially distinguished or important. When confronted with this memorandum recently, as a contradiction to what he was then saying, Mr. Acheson's only defense was that that State Department had been lying when the memorandum was sent out, in order to save face if Formosa did fall, and that lying was an acceptable instrument of diplomatic policy under such circumstances.

MacArthur has made his contrary views only too plain for the pro-Soviet group. In his statement about Formosa some eighteen months ago which the Administration tried to suppress, he said that the occupation of Formosa by Communist forces would be a direct threat to the security of the Pacific area and to the United States forces performing their lawful and necessary functions in that area. And he reemphasized this point of view in his speech to the joint session of Congress.

Since 1945 we have seen Poland, Hungary, Roumania, Albania, Bulgaria, Yugoslavia, Czecho-Slovakia, Manchuria, North Korea, and China lost to Stalin's agents. As a Brooklyn paper said not long ago: It is impossible to believe that stupidity alone has brought this about.

Many men have fought against it: Lane, Berle, Grew, Hurley, Wedemeyer, Clay, Forrestal, and others. Many were men of unusual courage, ability, and prestige. But none had the combination of these qualities necessary to overcome the opposition. MacArthur alone had been successful, up to three months ago, in his part of the world, in holding the Communists back — both in their political and their military efforts. So MacArthur had to be removed.

Many men have spearheaded these policies which were concocted of stupidity and treason in various degrees of combination. We could mention many names here, too, but it is better to omit them. But one man has led all the rest, and that man is Dean Acheson. I do not say that Acheson is a traitor. I do not claim to know his motivation. But by his own expressions of creed and purposes he is an extremely leftwing socialist. The facts make clear that under his increasing sway over our State Department and our whole government, the traitors and their dupes and allies have reached a terrifying position of influence and power. At the best we must put him down as a leader, friend, and protector of these dupes and allies.

In Europe Mr. Acheson has had his way almost completely. The mess we find ourselves in there is too horrible for contemplation. Nobody even wants to fight the Communists. Our former allies want us to fight them and to pay them huge bribes not to go over to the other side. The Germans hate us and ridicule us. On the mainland of Asia Mr. Acheson has had his way. Manchuria and China have been handed over to the Communists, Formosa and the Philippines are already threatened. Only in Japan has Acheson not had his way, and there only because of MacArthur. The record speaks for itself.

VII
SOURCES AND OPINIONS

This is already a long letter, and still I am afraid it cannot stop here. Up to this point it has been, except for one or two interpolations due to more recent events, almost exactly the speech which I delivered in Portland – of which you saw a very brief report. I had already made the same speech before several other groups, during April. I wish that I could have continued making it, and others I was also making concerning the rapid socialization of our country. But there are personal loyalties and obligations which cannot be ignored. And developments during May made the compulsion of these personal loyalties, to give up political activities for the sake of such heavy other demands on my time, even stronger than the patriotic obligation to keep my voice in the fight. Reluctantly but definitely I have given up all political efforts, even speechmaking, except such as might be proper for any business man and conscientious citizen with a normal interest in good government and public affairs. And this is one reason why I have written you at such length. For I have hoped that, by giving copies of this letter to a few good friends, I might have it serve in some degree to take the place of speeches I should like to make, as my small contribution to a better understanding of the dangers which we face.

When presenting this review verbally, with an audience in front of me, it has been easy to put in "asides" at the proper places, giving the sources of specific statements and quotations. But to have inserted "As Victor Lasky says" or some similar form of documentation, at every spot where it might reasonably be called for in this narrative, would have

41

encumbered it beyond the point of easy readability. For I wish to repeat that I have only been arranging and rearranging secondhand material.

To give now anything resembling a bibliography of sources would also give a pretense of scholarship, which is the last thing I wish to claim for this effort. But I cannot, with any feeling of honesty, simply ignore the problem altogether. So as humbly as possible I still want to make clear, without any footnote type of formality, at least some of the places where I have found pieces of information that went into this patchwork fabric.

In the first place, I can say honestly that I do read more socialist and Communist publications than anybody else I happen personally to know. And much of the background for this letter has been gathered from the outpourings of the enemy. But among "friendly" sources for such background, of people and personalities involved, I should give particular credit to Marjorie Shearon (*Challenge To Socialism*), Benjamin Gitlow (*The Whole Of Their Lives*), Jacob Spolansky (*The Communist Trail In America*), Robert E. Stripling (*The Red Plot Against America*), and, for my original instruction in Communist plotters and their ways, to that tremendously earnest idealist, Eugene Lyons (*Assignment In Utopia* and *The Red Decade*). For reference, the official publications of the House Un-American Activities Committee are always useful. And of course the newspapers and news magazines have been full of grist for this particular mill for years; the job is only to pick out and assemble what is wanted.

For the story primarily of events and incidents, rather than persons, Dr. Hollington Tong's *Dateline China* has been helpful. Speeches by Senator William E. Jenner and Congressman Walter Judd have been very much to the point. Copies of broadcasts by Henry J. Taylor have contained some nuggets which I have extracted. Kenneth de Courcy's *Intelligence Digest* is a periodical gold mine of accurate information on all foreign affairs. A pamphlet, *America Betrayed*, by Joseph Kamp, put out by the Constitutional Educational League, Inc., has served as a guide for running down connections between groups and individuals, and I have quoted from it almost directly in some places. And the thirteen-hundred-page publication of the State Department itself, *A Decade of American Foreign Policy*, would seem to me to offer sufficient evidence for any jury to convict at least Acheson's clique in the State Department of at least criminal stupidity.

From these and literally hundreds of newspaper clippings and other sources, I put together my speech as well as I could. But there was one source so much more important than any other that I have waited to mention it last. That was the brilliant collection of sheer facts and direct quotations compiled by Victor Lasky, in a small brochure called *The Case Against Dean Acheson*. In a couple of sections of this letter I have drawn very heavily on Lasky's essay, not even materially changing his wording at many points because no change would be an improvement. I am not in the least afraid of any characters in this story suing me for libel, for in order to do so they would have to subject themselves to cross examination under oath. They also would thus bring about a much wider reading of copies of this letter, which is the last thing most of them would want. But if Victor Lasky sues me for plagiarism I can hardly blame him, except that I am giving him blanket credit right now for practically anything he wishes to claim in about a third of these pages. And certainly we are both toilers in the same vineyard. If you want further evidence, read the marvelous book, as interesting as any mystery novel, called *The Seeds Of Treason*, by Lasky and Toledano, published by Funk & Wagnalls. It is the story of the Alger Hiss trials, and will help to open your eyes.

In your own letter you said that you hated to see me jumping on the Martin-Wherry-MacArthur bandwagon. I hope

I have convinced you at least that I was not jumping on anybody's bandwagon; that my thoughts and feelings on this subject were entirely too deep for any such purpose. You brought forth, especially in the copy of your letter to newspaper editors, a number of arguments supporting the Acheson policies against those of MacArthur. It would take too much additional space for me to try to set forth my differing opinions with regard to these various points, and I want to comment on only one. You rather ridicule the idea of our thinking Asiatic territory is important enough to Stalin for us to fight over it with any sizable proportion of our forces, and express the belief that Stalin is trying to trap us into committing large amounts of our war potential to Asia so that he can grab off Europe more easily. Maybe so. But if so, it is contrary to everything we know about the plans of Russian imperialism, dating back to the dreams of the Czars, which is the only thing the Soviets have taken over, lock, stock and barrel, from the Russian past. The idea that the conquest of Asia, or at least China, had to precede the conquest of Europe, has been a cardinal tenet of Soviet foreign policy from the time they first went to work on China within three years of their original revolution. "The road to Paris is through Peiping" is the way they have put it time and time again, for the guidance of their own party-thinking, and their actions have shown clearly how firmly Stalin and the other Soviet leaders have believed in this long-range strategy themselves.

You said you thought this MacArthur storm was just the kind of false-trail issue which the Republicans habitually picked up, causing them to lose elections, and which, unless they abandoned it promptly, would cause them to lose the 1952 election. And that you were greatly concerned with having Republicans take courses that would enable them to win.

For one thing, I believe you are wrong in your appraisal of

the issue. There are three broad areas of argument in which the 1952 political battle can be waged. One is corruption in government, one is the steady encroachment of socialism, and one is foreign policy. An honest fight for principles will require the Republicans to hammer away on all three fronts, rather than try to take some slick position which they think is politically smart. But from the point of view of political strategy, the great opportunity lies in the third field. For the more than two million Federal office holders and their families, not as a rule feeling strongly enough about corruption in government to throw overboard their own personal stakes in a Democratic victory, can exert a balance of power that is hard to overcome. And the blessings of the handout-state reach too many favored segments of our population for it to be easy to recruit enough revolting individualists from the Democratic ranks. But let these same people, office holders and beneficiaries of New Deal class legislation alike, become convinced that the policies of this administration are really endangering their country, and they will push aside less important matters of self-interest in a stampede to throw out the bunglers, the crooks, and the traitors who have brought us to such a pass. There is no conceivable issue which could so quickly bring the best elements of the Democratic party over in droves, to at least temporary support of Republican leadership, as a conviction that a sizable part of Democratic officialdom was playing directly into Russia's hands. And I believe that the material to convince them of this fact is plentiful and irrefutable, if the Republicans will only have the courage and the straight-forwardness to pick it up and use it.

But there is an even more important point that I want to make in this connection. I am a good Republican. And as I have said many times before, I think that the Republican Party is the one practical instrumentality which offers any chance of a return in this country to more honesty and sanity in government and more common sense in our economic thinking. I too am greatly concerned over the need of a Republican victory. But the impact of what is happening in Washington, and of the devious game our State Department is playing in so many parts of the world, transcends even these soundest reasons for my strong partisanship. Rather than cease to fight the dangerous machinations of the Acheson clique at every turn, in whatever small way my own restricted circumstances will permit, I would abandon the Republican Party in a minute. And I shall try to make my reasons clearer in the concluding section of this letter.

VIII
SOME GENERAL PREMISES

It is now July 14 — Bastille Day, just by chance. It is the anniversary of that day, one hundred and sixty-two years ago, which was supposed to inaugurate freedom from tyranny forevermore.

Writing this letter, in snatches of time that I could spare, has not been any fun. For in the course of my fifty-one years I have learned that the man in whom you see only the bad side today may prove to be a good man fighting on your side tomorrow. I am well aware that the molasses of debating issues catches more favorable attention than the vinegar of personal criticisms. And neither my judgment nor my deep-rooted sense of good will towards my fellow man will let me assume the role of bitter critic of individuals without misgivings and reluctance. But it is exactly this civilized tolerance, and the charity of our Christian outlook, that the Communists are counting on, and using ruthlessly, as one of their strongest weapons. When personalities as well as issues become of the very essence of a movement, and that movement seeks our total destruction, it is cowardice and not fairmindedness to skirt around the names of those who are used by the enemy.

Writing the rest of this letter will be even less fun, because honesty will require that I appear as an alarmist. And it is an obviously wise generalization that an alarmist seldom gets anybody excited except himself. I can write these remaining pages as I do only because I am frankly and deeply frightened. And with every paragraph I shall be hoping, but not believing, that the extent of my fright is not really justified.

For we can begin this conclusion with certain definite premises which seem, to me at least, to be factually established beyond all doubt.

The first is that the Soviet leaders are, without exception, murderers, liars, thieves, and ruthlessly cruel tyrants. I do not mean these words to be mere epithets, but specific and accurate descriptions. Their very dogma has for three decades made virtues of these characteristics, and only those members of the Communist party who are unhesitatingly capable of using any foulness to achieve an end have any chance whatsoever of rising to positions of leadership. The lives and the suffering of millions of Chinese or of millions of Ukrainian kulaks or of miscellaneous millions of their slave labor battalions mean no more to Stalin or Mao or Molotov or Malik than the lives and suffering of millions of ants.

We hear a great deal about Americans having lost their sense of moral values, and their capacity for indignation at the manifest and brazen corruption in our governments. Unfortunately, there is much truth to the accusation. But to my mind even this sign of moral degeneration is not nearly so disturbing as our calm acceptance of the barbaric brutalities of Communist monsters everywhere. These men are not human beings, they are predatory beasts; atavisms throwing back to the days of the Assyrians, constantly engaging without the slightest shame in bestialities that the human race thought it had outgrown and left behind with the fall of Nineveh eighty generations ago.

47

The second premise is that the Communist inner circle has never wavered, and will never waver in the slightest or for an instant, in its determination to conquer and rule the world; and that Stalin thoroughly expects, within his lifetime, to make slaves, completely subject to his personal power, of every human being on the planet. His obsession with this epic ambition is the only possible explanation of a thousand different procedures that have unrolled right before our eyes. This megalomaniacal dream on the part of imaginative tyrants has been one of the horrible factors in the sociological currents of the past fifty years. It must be charged on the debit side, in appraisal of that rapid decrease in the size of our world brought about by scientific wonders in transportation and communications.

The third premise is that Stalin and his subordinates will use every means, of treachery, of diplomacy, of propaganda, of murderous liquidation of millions of potential enemies, of military destructiveness, of outlawed methods of warfare, of temporary compromise, of fifth-column infiltration, of carefully fomented confusion, and of recruiting power-seeking Quislings to his standard in every country, to achieve this ambition. We see every single one of these means being widely used, or in preparation for use — even to bacteriological warfare — already as visible and incontrovertible facts.

The fourth premise is that Communist infiltration into our government, and the recruiting and planting of Communist traitors in spots of vital control in every important branch of our economic, political, and cultural life, has already gone far beyond the wildest guess of the average American citizen. Documentation of this fact is so easy and so simple that even I could put together a letter longer than this one full of nothing but names and incidents to support it. The Communists themselves have boasted that their organization in this country is like a submerged submarine; we see only the periscope. In the article in the July 14 issue of the *Saturday*

Evening Post, concerning conferences in Moscow in July, 1947, in which the Czech, Arnhost Heidrich, participated, the two most significant sentences are these: "Heidrich sensed that Stalin believed deeply that the American Government was not really master in its own house. He, Stalin, was the real master of the situation." And Whittaker Chambers accurately complained that the personal drama of the Hiss trial had served to divert attention from the really important part of the picture, which was the magnitude of the Communist conspiracy in this country.

Fifth, the smoke screen thrown up to keep us from getting a clear look at even the periscope of this Communist apparatus is becoming constantly thicker, darker, and more difficult to penetrate. (1) The traitors and their dupes and allies belch it out in unceasing volume; (2) the whole power of the Truman administration is used as a bellows to blow it in the directions most needed; (3) the you-scratch-my-back-I-scratch-your-back socialists cooperate with their Communist friends, frequently not even beginning to realize how they are being used, to add their tens of thousands of little black clouds; (4) and even our good American newspapers, feeling that they must constantly be proving how "liberal" and "tolerant" they are, dim their searchlights or turn them the other way.

(1) There reached my desk today a new book by the same IPR crowd, published in 1951, for which I paid five dollars. The list of authors of its different chapters, and of more than forty authors of books on Asia in general, or on China specifically, referred to in its bibliography, reads like a *Who's Who* among Communists and fellow travelers connected with the sell-out of Chiang Kai-shek. I opened the book at random, to Page 32, and read that much as a sample of the whole that I would get to later. I have never seen as much or as clever distortion of the facts, or net falsification of a record, in any other one page of anything called history. Yet

this book of several hundred pages looks completely plausible to anybody who has not taken the trouble to dig below the surface of pro-Communist propaganda.

(2) When the Un-American Activities Committee was investigating the Whittaker Chambers charges against Alger Hiss, the greatest worry of Representative Nixon and other members of the Committee was that the United States Department of Justice would succeed in putting a stop to the investigation, or to any charges against Hiss, even after the Department had impounded sixty-five documents substantiating Chambers' charges. President Truman has insisted that investigations of Communist activities were "red herrings," and let the full power of his office be used to hamstring them. A long letter from the F.B.I. concerning the extended Communist associations of one high government officer has been highhandedly withheld by Truman despite a ten-to-one Congressional vote demanding its release. The State Department, denying at every turn that there were any pro-Communists in its ranks, and fighting every disclosure, still was forced to drop 151 people from its payroll for subversive activities in a twenty-four-month period; and has still gone on hiring, protecting, and promoting pro-Communists with greater fervor than ever. Since the first seven sections of this letter were written the State Department, apparently in fear of actions of the McCarran Committee, has suspended, as a "poor security risk," that same John P. Davies, referred to far above, who had been fired from Chungking by Pat Hurley, as a pro-Communist, in 1945. In the meantime he had continued under Dean Acheson, for all the years in between, to be "a member of Secretary of State Acheson's top level policy planning staff." Dropped with him for similar reasons at the same time was another notorious character, Oliver Edmund Clubb, who was, significantly, Director of the Office of China Affairs. It is reported that the records of some fifty others are being "re-examined." But you can bet your bottom dollar

that they will all be replaced by others of the same ilk — and that most of them will again wind up somewhere in the State Department. More important, and pertinent to these immediate paragraphs, is that neither you nor any government committee will ever be able to learn one-tenth of what they may have done to forward the Communist cause.

(3) Not too long ago a left-wing opportunist, Avedis Boghos Derounian, was being sued for libel. Under one of his many aliases, John Roy Carlson, he had written a book called *Under Cover*, full of vicious smears about many good and patriotic Americans. The purport of his book, and basis for his smears, was that anybody who opposed Communists or Communism, or who could even be remotely connected with those who opposed Communism, was a Fascist conspirator. At the end of this particular trial the respectable presiding judge felt impelled to go further than merely awarding damages to the plaintiff. He gave a tongue-lashing to the publisher, stating that a man who would publish such a book would do anything for money. Yet, thanks to widespread and favorable reviews, that book sold over seven hundred thousand copies.

We have heard a great deal about Communist infiltration in Hollywood. It has actually become domination rather than infiltration. The F.B.I. has the names of thirty-three *card-bearing* Communists in the very top echelons of the movie headquarters — directors, authors, and writers. There are at least one hundred and fifty of these top-flight movie people who have shown themselves by their actions to be strongly sympathetic to the Stalinist conspiracy. The fact that it was intellectually fashionable, *and so much easier to get to the top* in Hollywood if you were a sympathizer, had a great deal to do with drawing so many into the net.

The same thing is true of so many other fields of work which involve media for influencing American public opinion, including the book-reviewing profession. There are today hopeful signs of a return to more fairmindedness and objectivity in some quarters such as the *New York Times.* There are plenty of able, informed, patriotic, and objective book reviewers still left, of course, just as there are still many "movie greats" untouched by the Communist brush; but they have both been carrying a heavy handicap load. During recent years, in the book-review columns of the *Times,* the *New York Herald Tribune*, the *Saturday Review of Literature*, and the *New Republic,* people like Agnes Smedley, Edgar Snow, John K. Fairbank, Owen Lattimore, Annalee Jacoby and their kind have played to the hilt the game of praising each other's books — with front pages in the book sections and ample space conveniently provided them; and of tearing down, when they could not manage to have the publications completely ignored, such books as W.L. White's *Report on the Russians*, or George Creel's *Russia's Race for Asia,* or Freda Utley's *Last Chance in China.* The fact that Lewis Gannett, book review editor of the *Herald Tribune*, has been mentioned seventeen times by the House Un-American Activities Committee as among the subjects of their investigation is revealing. As is his free plug for the literary efforts of Mr. Howard Fast — since sentenced to jail for refusing to tell Congress whether or not he was a Communist.

These top-flight pinks set the pace, largely for ideological or long-range conspiratorial purposes. But the plain matter of personal prestige and of making a living reinforces the pressure all down the line. The book to which I referred in (1) will go on to get huge and grand reviews. For it has long been clear even to the lesser lights that the way to win big reputations as book reviewers, and the emoluments such reputations bring, is to turn out favorable reviews at every chance of this kind. The way to get smeared, and called an ignorant hack — and ultimately to be out of work — is to give this book .a poor — or an honest — review. With the help of wide and favorable reviews the book will go on to attain a huge sale, and to be placed in every sizable library in the country; and to make a lot of money for its publisher. There are hundreds of such books flooding the country all of the time. I ordered two more just today. One of them, at five dollars, with an extremely solid-sounding historical title, is by a man who, despite his innocent sounding name being completely unknown to the average unsuspecting reader, has been an active and ardent Communist sympathizer, on three continents and for many years.

(4) Right up practically till the time Alger Hiss was finally convicted and sentenced, the *Boston Herald* was blasting away editorially at those foul witch-hunting bigots beneath contempt who were low enough to persecute such a noble American as Alger Hiss. It was already perfectly obvious, to anybody who would take the trouble to study the known evidence objectively, that Hiss was a particularly cunning and vindictive liar, who was using every dirty trick he knew to forward the Communist cause. But this editorial was typical of the kind of press that everybody has had to face who has tried to penetrate the smoke screen. The *Boston Herald* is one of our better newspapers, which is why I selected it for this illustration instead of such mouthpieces of bias as the *Washington Post* or the *Raleigh News And Observer*. It certainly has not been infiltrated by pro-Communists. And as a general rule — except possibly when it goes on a specific political binge — the *Herald* presents "conservative" and "liberal" news and columnists in a fair degree of balance. But at least some of its editorial writers constantly feel that they must flaunt their "liberalism" by making it as uncomfortable as possible for anybody trying to get at the truth about a Hiss, a Remington, or "Doctors" Jessup and Lattimore.

Here again I have picked up just a few tiny straws for illustration, out of a haystack the size of a mountain. Here again even I could fill a hundred pages with names and incidents exactly to the point. But I must move towards the end.

A sixth premise is that Stalin, at long last, is approaching the position where he will be willing to add war to the other means he has so far been using. Up till now he has taken over country after country by treason within; in many cases, such as those of Poland and China, with the active help and connivance of the Truman administration and our State Department. He was neither able, ready, nor willing to risk the actual use of armed forces. And at any step within the past five years he could have been stopped cold by a firm show of force in the place of the constant and even anxious appeasement which was offered him.

The idiocies that the American people have been sold by the State Department since 1944 are legion. But no other idiocy, not even that of the Mao Communists being "agrarian reformers," has quite approached the brazen duplicity of the continuously repeated excuse that Stalin must be allowed to have his way, in one grab and one breach of agreement and one murderous betrayal of our friends after another, because otherwise he might start a third world war. It was known to anybody with the slightest powers of observation that neither agreements nor moral scruples nor any civilized consideration would hold Stalin back from war when he was ready for war; that nothing would provoke him into war until he was ready; and that if he were ready for war he would already be fighting. It was Stalin's time table that we were following, and Stalin to whom we were giving needed time, rather than ourselves.

But now time is running out. Thanks to the Allan Nunn Mays, the Klaus Fuchses, the Pontecorvos, the Rosenbergs, and all the treason of which they were only the tiny part that has been exposed, Stalin now has the atom bomb. The private intelligence authority that disclosed several months ahead just when the Russians would explode their first test bomb, and which announced the explosion to the world the very day it happened, says that Stalin is and for a long time has been stockpiling atom bombs at the rate of four a month; and that he is considerably ahead of us in development of the hydrogen bomb. That same authority, which has not once been wrong in a period of years, states categorically that in less than twenty-four months Stalin will have all of Iran's oil.[15] He has German scientists adding to his huge fleet of advanced-type submarines, building jet engines for his airplanes, and developing all other deadly weapons that have so far been conceived. Through his lieutenant Mao he has conquered mainland China, the first great nation, and source of unending manpower, to be added to his resources. His agents are everywhere; in Cuba there are known to be more than fifty thousand Communists; in Panama they have operated so successfully, according to Hallett Abend, "that today the Panama Canal is admittedly indefensible"; the amount of Communist strength in Hawaii has already paralyzed the islands twice in four years. In South and Central America there are now half a million Communist agents, under the disciplined control of the infamous Jan Drohojowski. In our own country there is now, according to J. Edgar Hoover, one Communist (actual party member) for every 1814 persons, against one Communist for every 2277 persons in Russia at the time they overthrew the Russian government. And their power is magnified out of all proportion to their numbers by the help of their dupes and allies, and by the strategic positions in which they have put themselves.

Time is running out. The strongest indication of this is that Stalin has already had his rehearsal, which is such a cardinal point in his cunning practicality. As he explained to Winston Churchill, it is necessary "to blood your troops" before the big trial comes. He fomented and used the Spanish Civil War as a testing ground for weapons and a training ground for guerilla troops, in advance of the war with Hitler that he knew was on the way.

Stalin obviously wanted us to fight back in Korea, for the same purpose. (To put it bluntly, we would not have fought in Korea if Stalin had wished otherwise. We pulled our troops out of South Korea because he wanted us to. We announced that we would not defend Korea because he wanted us to. We ignored the clearest repeated warnings of the forthcoming attack, because he wanted us to, until the very day he struck. And we reversed our position and fought back, after getting the odds stacked against ourselves in every imaginable way, because he wanted us to, and pulled the strings. *You* find any other conceivable explanation.) He wanted a chance to test his jet planes and other engines of war, and to "blood" his Asiatic troops in battles with Western soldiery. Undoubtedly he expected to wipe us off the peninsula in easy order, adding terrific prestige to his bluff of invincibility in arms, and giving his Chinese soldiers, and their Russian advisors and bosses, a terrific boost in confidence. That this did not work out quite as expected was due to the independent Americanism of MacArthur, the daring military genius of MacArthur which conceived and executed the Inchon landing, and the courage of the vastly outnumbered men under him. But even then Stalin was sure enough of being master within our house not to run any real risk. He could ensure that his troops and planes fought from protected sanctuaries; and that, if and whenever he thought it best, all he had to do was to consent to stop the war, on terms which would still be a disgrace to America and could readily be sold as a huge Communist victory by his Asiatic propaganda machines. Our representatives marching with a white flag into a formal assemblage of armed Communists, in a spot held by the Communists below the 38th parallel, to have their pictures thus taken for dissemination all over Asia, proved how well-founded was his assurance. The peace terms eventually to be worked out will prove it even more disgracefully. The one and only thing that had to be done, to bring this about – and to avoid the possibility that the United States forces might actually and eventually stop fighting with their hands tied behind their backs – was the removal of MacArthur. The rehearsal is now over. Despite seventy thousand American casualties, the most important single result has been a devastation of a friendly country, so severe and so complete as to furnish terrific propaganda to Stalin's agents everywhere else concerning the folly of resistance.

Time is running out. Evidence is piling up on many sides and from many sources that October, 1952, is the fatal month when Stalin will attack. I should like to explore that evidence, too, but it would take an additional several pages. I must go on to my seventh, and last, premise.[14, 16]

The war that Stalin will begin when ready will be totally unlike anything this country or any other great nation has ever faced before. It will be external war, bacteriological war and war with every civilized rule as to uniforms or prisoners or decency of any kind thrown completely overboard by our enemy. It will use the murder of civilian millions, by firing squads behind the lines, as a routine instrument of conquest. It will begin with A-bombs exploding at vital centers, catastrophic sabotage of railroads, airlines, and industrial plants, and a simultaneous seizure of power in many spots by armed fifth columnists. Robert Stripling, who spent ten thankless years exposing Communist traitors in this country, and who did expose a great many despite every obstacle these traitors and their dupes and allies in various government departments could put in his way, says: "It is incontrovertible that every key point, strategically, in the United States has been studied faithfully against the day when peaceful-looking American Reds will be called upon to come into the open and fight for Mother Russia."

In expectation of that approaching day the Quislings in

our midst are already getting more brazen, more arrogant, and more confident. For they feel that they have to hang on only so much longer. Then *they* will be the government and you and I will be the traitors to that government. Treason has to prosper only so far and then none dare call it treason. We are already dangerously near that edge. Alarmism? Merciful heavens, my good friend and good fellow American, look in front of you. This has been happening right before your eyes. It happened in the Ukraine. It happened in Poland, in Rumania, in Hungary, in Czecho-Slovakia. In many of these places, God forgive us, we have helped it to happen. Every trustworthy report we get out of China tells us of the thousands who are being murdered in cold blood every day. The total, before the purge is finished, will be many times the huge number of Chinese our soldiers killed in the Korean war. One estimate, by a pro-Communist, of the troops and civilians combined that have already been killed by the Mao forces, is "in the neighborhood of 14,000,000."

I happened to be in Paris the day Czecho-Slovakia fell, a little over three years ago. As a result, the impact of that tragic fall was much greater on me than if I had been in Belmont, Massachusetts. The Czechs were not poverty-stricken Chinese, nor unlettered Ukrainian peasants, nor nomadic tribes of some non-industrialized wasteland. They were among the most civilized, hardest working, most law-abiding, best educated people in all of Europe. And they were so sure that "it couldn't happen to them." They were playing the game sensibly. They had liberalized and broadened their government; they had taken in the Communists, in a proper Democratic way, and even had a Communist deputy premier and other Communist officials mixed in with their ministers of other parties. They were recovering prosperity, not rapidly but surely. And the future looked glorious ahead, as such wisdom deserved. Or so they believed, and boasted, of all these things, right up till the hour the blow struck. The rest is history, from which we well might learn.

The seventh and last premise is that the allies, on whom we are supposedly depending so much as to let our policies be swayed by their desires and fears, are even more vulnerable to the Soviet fifth column than we are ourselves, in either a hot war or a continued cold one. Just a few comments about the British picture will have to suffice, to indicate the substantiation of this premise which would be possible in a separate letter on the subject.

Most of the effective thefts of atomic bomb secrets from our laboratories and archives have been achieved by men who were passed as security risks by the *British government*, and allowed their opportunities by our government supposedly on the strength of this British clearance. Allan Nunn May, Klaus Fuchs, and Pontecorvo were all whitehaired boys of the *British* government. There is other and ample evidence that the permeation of actual spies and traitors into the British government has exceeded their boring into ours. Within the past few weeks this fact has been highlighted again by the disappearance, obviously behind the Iron Curtain, of MacLean and Burgess. Despite the fact that MacLean was known to have been associated with the Communist Party in England at one time, he was Chief of the American Department in the British Foreign Office. He had access to, and knowledge of, a tremendous number of top secret communications, not all necessarily connected with his department. Burgess, though a lesser light, was also known to have had dangerous Communist associations. Yet, just as in *hundreds* of similar situations in both the British government and ours, these men had been allowed to stay in positions where espionage, much of it at the very top level, was extremely easy. When they first disappeared in France, somebody in the British government fumbled or *deliberately withheld* passing this information on to the French government until too late; until MacLean and Burgess had been shuffled behind the Iron Curtain. And the British government has made every effort it could to keep the facts about this whole occurrence from being exposed. Shades of *Amerasia*! Lord Vansittart has recently stated that a very large number of pro-Communist officials are in the government; that they protect each other and use their official influence to keep anybody from giving the full facts about the Soviet to the public; that the extent of Communist influence is immense; and that Russia's friends and agents are placed in key positions. There are plenty of other authorities to support Lord Vansittart's allegations; but there are extremely powerful forces to prevent anything being done about them.

In 1939 the British Labor Party was an extremely left-wing organization. Yet at conventions held specifically for that purpose, in the fall of 1939 and the spring of 1940, Sir Stafford Cripps, Aneurin Bevan, and G.R. Strauss were kicked completely out of the Labor Party as being too pro-Communist even for that group. They did not get back in the party until 1944. But when the Socialists came to power in 1945 these men became perhaps the three most powerful in the government, and remained so for several years. John Strachey was once held up at Ellis Island and refused admission to the United States as a Communist. He claims to have abandoned *Russian* Communism in 1940, but is not so positive about communism as an ideology or as it might be spelled with a little "c". Strachey has been Minister of War in the British cabinet for most of the years of Russia's great expansion. At least one other British cabinet officer is notorious for his known *former* Communist sympathies.

As for the extent to which treason in England has already prospered, to the point where it dares come right out in the open and brazenly defy anybody to call it treason, please note this: Less than a month ago an official representative of the British Foreign Office stated in a public speech that *South* Korea had started the fighting, and that the only aggressor in the Far East was America. Time is truly running out!

Those who believe that there is anything unduly alarmist about any of these lines have my hopes and prayers that they are right. But the evidence otherwise is like the light of a noonday sun.

IX
CONCLUSION

And now finally, in about two pages, I shall be through. I return to your original letter, and the firing of MacArthur. It is my utterly sincere belief that, through whatever strings may have been pulled and whatever puppets activated to exert their combined insidious pressures, MacArthur was fired by Stalin. He had to be removed. Otherwise he might have ultimately had his way, and have blown the Chinese Communists and their supply bases right off the Manchurian landscape. Chiang Kai-shek was in position to do it once, and truces were forced on him, by American diplomatic pressures, to prevent it. Diplomacy is a wonderful thing if you own all the diplomats on one side and a sufficient number on the other.

The next American obstacle on the Communist schedule to be removed is undoubtedly J. Edgar Hoover. Hamstrung as the F.B.I. is by being an adjunct of the highly political Justice Department, and discouraged and frustrated as the F.B.I. men feel on having their most carefully substantiated investigations of Communist subversives ignored when prosecutions are sought, the F.B.I. so far is still in position to pick up about 25,000 known Communist agents in this country on short notice. This is a powerful threat to their strength which the Communists cannot ignore. Whatever its significance may be, it is worth noting that a little over a year ago one of Dean Acheson's former law partners began circulating a petition demanding as "imperative in the public interest"

61

that there be a public investigation of the "lawless conduct of the F.B.I." Perhaps this maneuver was found to be premature. In the face of rising criticism the attack was turned off. But there have been others, such as the viciously distorted book by Max Lowenthal, a White House favorite. And that there will be new ones, more aggressively continued, you can be sure.

For all my pessimism as to the prospects ahead of us, I have no doubt as to the ultimate outcome. However crippled America may be, by traitors inside and by the destructiveness of the external enemy, I am sure that the shattered remnant of our people and of our industrial and military might will be able to rise, fight, and coalesce, and win. But it is the cost, the so bitterly unnecessary cost, of victory in such wise, that makes me shudder as though in a horrible nightmare. And the unbroken trend of events but makes that nightmare worse.

Every time we allow a Grew or a Dooman, a Berle or a Lane to be pushed out of their path by the Soviet conspirators we are just making the eventual holocaust that much more certain and more deadly. I believe, as do many others, that a sufficiently firm stand could still stop Stalin, at this terribly late hour, short of the fatal plunge; that not his intentions, but at least his time-schedule, could be disrupted simply by our beginning to show, by actions and words, that we recognize as beasts rather than men the monsters who control the Soviet tyranny, and by our taking steps to protect ourselves in accordance with this realization. I believe, as do many others, that any such show of ordinary hard-headedness and determination on our part would inspire spasmodic but increasing insurrections against this tyranny, in the satellite countries and even within the so-called Soviet republics themselves; and that even moral support from us, which could be depended on, might well be sufficient to encourage a revolt of growing strength, sufficient at last to send the whole Stalinist hierarchy fleeing like frightened dogs in search of hiding places. So far we have actually helped to betray millions and millions of decent people who would have been glad to fight on our side. The removal of a man like MacArthur, aside from depriving us of one of our ablest soldiers in either the cold war or a hot one, is notice to all these would-be friends that the Soviet plotters are masters of our government today, just as they were masters of the governments within the countries of these friends long before such mastery became official. And to allow Dean Acheson to remain as Secretary of State, with the other positions of official as well as unofficial influence in our government which he also holds, is under present circumstances like allowing a precocious child to play with matches and firecrackers, wherever he pleases, in the various departments of a huge powder factory.

Communism as an ideology is just one of Stalin's tools. With it, and with the more direct methods of a ruthless organization that stops at nothing, he is tearing down our civilized world so as to stand astride it. He is doing so just when American production methods, spreading throughout an unregimented and uncurtained world, could have brought an increasing measure of personal freedom and a gradually rising standard of living to individuals everywhere. What is happening right before our eyes is by far the greatest tragedy in the history of mankind. The danger which is so imminently confronting America, and the malignity of the force now doing incalculable ruin, piece by piece, in a world to which America now owes leadership, transcend all questions of the Republican Party against the Democratic Party, or of political advantage. But it took nine years for Whittaker Chambers to get anybody in our government to listen to his story and do anything about it. As was wisely written a long time ago, there are none so blind as those who will not see.

Sincerely,

ROBERT H.W. WELCH, JR.

A Postscript

February 22, 1952

Dear Mr. Regnery:

Publication of this paper, to meet the demand for copies, has become a necessity. And I am grateful for your confidence and courage, in putting on it the imprint of your company and in taking the business risk involved.

But it is still with deep regret that I see the treatise published in this form. It is such a fragmentary and unfinished work. As it changes status, from an informal letter duplicated by friends, to a semi-historical essay given the dignity of print, there is so much more that needs to be said to round out the picture.

For the preceding pages delineate a pattern that has been repeated since Teheran like the design in a piece of wallpaper. With a few changes in names and dates the story becomes that of Poland or of Yugoslavia. It is conceivable that the fortuitous interplay of political, diplomatic, and military forces could produce in one country, such as China, an improbable tragedy. But when remarkably parallel developments have produced remarkably similar catastrophes in other parts of the world; when the same identical methods of deception, betrayal, and brutality, speeded by the same acceptance and even well-timed support by agencies of our government, have been successful in country after country; when our aid to an aggressive tyrant, defended even at the best as opportunistic appeasement, has followed so regular a form that its course can be charted in advance; in the light of such experience it is not unreasonable to ask just how far the long arm of coincidence can reach. As we have moved from openly "helping our Soviet ally" to "containment of Communism" to "standing up against Stalin," only the phrases have been altered. As to the direction of the forces working behind the scenes, and as to the results achieved by these forces year after year, the plain present facts tell a story there is no refuting. In some manner, made inexplicable by a planned confusion, even our steps of supposed resistance — such as Korea — work out to be victories for the Kremlin. Never has there been a better illustration of the old French proverb that the more it changes the more it is just the same thing.

There is no change in the Communist formula of conquest, nor in the variables — one of which is always our assistance — manipulated by that formula. The only change is in the coefficients of those variables. I tried hard, in the long letter, to define that formula by tracing its application to China. I had hoped and planned to try just as hard, in other long letters, to make the formula a great deal more obvious by recounting its exactly similar application to other countries.

But one man can do only so much, and my responsibilities over the past many months have been varied and heavy. Now the definite publication plans mean that time has closed in on me, and maybe space as well. I am going to find *some* time, nevertheless, for a small part of what so badly needs to be added, and shall do my utmost to persuade you to find the necessary space. To avoid wasting either I shall plunge ahead.

II
POLAND GOES FIRST

In 1683, when John Sobieski, by lifting the siege of Vienna, saved much of Europe from being overrun by the

66

Turks, Poland was one of the great powers of the continent. But it had three weaknesses and dangers, the combination of which was gradually to prove fatal. One was that it was an *elective monarchy*, a contradiction in the logic of government which alone was disastrous. The second was a provision in the Polish constitution of a *liberum veto*, whereby any one member of parliament, even if openly bribed for that purpose by a foreign power, could prevent any action he didn't like by dissolving the parliament itself or by threatening to do so. (The origin of the *veto* in the United Nations charter lies, of course, in Stalin's familiarity with Polish history, and with the value of such a monkey wrench to be tossed at will into any governmental machinery.) The third was simply the brazen hunger of Poland's neighbors, especially Russia, for her territory.

Less than one hundred years later the combination of these corroding factors led to the first partition, whereby Poland lost, to Russia, Austria, and Prussia, one-fifth of her population and one-fourth of her area. By the second partition, in 1793, Poland was reduced to one-third of her original dimensions. And by the third partition among exactly the same powers, in 1796, Poland ceased to exist. Despite the ephemeral Grand Duchy of Warsaw, created by Napoleon and fought for with such futility by Poniatowski and his brave patriots, and despite the amorphous "Congress Kingdom" which had Russian Tsars as its sovereigns for fifty years, there was no nation of Poland again until Woodrow Wilson restored it, in 1919, through the Treaty of Versailles.

The first Premier was Ignace Paderewski, as good a friend of America as we ever had. The Poles, through all of their tumultuous history, have remained a proud, brave, and intensely nationalistic people. They were extremely appreciative of the part played by the United States, supported by England and France, in the re-establishment of their dismembered country. Friendship with these western republics, and distrust of both the Russian and German dictatorships, was the keynote of Polish foreign policy in the period between the two wars. Here again the sequel is made more sad by the fact that it was our best friends we betrayed. The fourth partition of Poland, between Stalin and Hitler in 1939, set off the Second World War. England entered the fight to back up its guarantee to Poland against such encroachment. The preservation of the national independence and established boundaries of Poland, and of any country similarly attacked by any tyrannical aggressor, was the high-sounding theme of the Atlantic Charter, under which we also edged our way into the holocaust. These facts make the sequel not only a greater tragedy, but an epic for the ages in the category of callous and cynical hypocrisy.

When Hitler broke his alliance with Stalin, and invaded Russia, his forces immediately overran all of Poland, including that part ceded to Russia in the partition of two years before. And the Germans held this Polish territory until very near the end of the war. But the Poles and their leaders never gave up fighting. A coalition Polish Government In Exile was established, at first in France and then in London. Led at first by Sikorski, until he was killed in an airplane accident in 1943, and then by Prime Minister Mikolajczyk, this government maintained close relations with the best and most effective underground resistance army in Europe, commanded in Poland by General Bor-Komorowski.

After Stalingrad the Germans began to retreat; and the Russians gradually followed, to the banks of the Vistula. On the other side, in Warsaw, were General Bor and two hundred and fifty thousand underground troops, awaiting the time and the word to break into open insurrection against their German conquerors. On July 30, 1944, General Bor's radio picked up a broadcast in Polish, from the Moscow radio, signed by Molotov. It said: "Poles, the time of liberation is at hand! Poles, to arms! Make every Polish home a stronghold against the invader. There is not a moment to lose!"

The next day a similar broadcast, from Moscow, was heard in London. Premier Mikolajczyk, who had been promised aid for the Warsaw insurrectionists by Stalin himself, immediately left for Moscow, and this fact was communicated to the Warsaw patriots. General Bor, believing that Russian military aid was at hand, gave the order to revolt.

The whole affair was, of course, a typically ruthless Stalin trap. The Russian army stopped advancing. While General Bor's guerilla forces fought with bravery never surpassed, but without tanks, airplanes, or heavy artillery, against fully equipped German units — and caused the complete demolishment of their great city of Warsaw in the process — Stalin refused even to allow airplanes to drop supplies which the insurgents so desperately needed.

Despite spectacular early successes, at the end of two months the whole Polish Home Army was completely annihilated. This of course had been the purpose of the ruse. For otherwise the patriots in that army might later have fought as valiantly against the Russian tyrant as they did against the German.

(This pitiless horror was part and parcel of that cruel farsightedness which had caused Stalin, five years before, to send to slave labor camps in Russia, from that part of Poland which the pact with Hitler had put in his hands, and while that pact lasted, 1,200,000 leading Polish citizens in mass deportations. These were the solid and substantial members of each community, who might later have caused him trouble. It was but a different variation of the Katyn Massacre, in which ten thousand captured Polish army officers, separated from their troops and concentrated in one group, were shot down in cold blood by bullets through the backs of their skulls, and their bodies piled in a huge mass grave in the forest near Smolensk. These trained and patriotic officers might later have been troublesome, too.)

In the meantime betrayal on the diplomatic front was more than keeping pace with betrayal on the military front.

69

On July 30, 1941, in the days of Stalin's great need after Hitler's attack, the Soviet Government had entered into a pact with the Polish Government In Exile, making the two nations allies against Germany. But even in this instrument Stalin had refused recognition[12] of Poland's 1939 boundaries; and Premier Sikorski, *under strong pressure from the British government*, and despite the resignation of several members of his cabinet over the matter, signed the pact without this provision being included. By early December, 1941, the Soviet Government was conscripting soldiers for its own army from Poland's eastern provinces, and stating that "the question of the frontier between the Soviet Union and Poland has not been settled and is subject to settlement in the future."

When Anthony Eden visited Moscow later that month Stalin was already claiming that part of Poland which he had taken, in the partition with Hitler, as permanently his own. And the British Government — which had gone to war ostensibly to protect Poland's boundaries — was already willing to concede Stalin's claim! That claim was held up temporarily by two patriotic career men in our State Department, James C. Dunn and Ray Atherton — both of whom have long since been pushed out. They got Secretary Hull to state flatly that the American Government would not accept any such Soviet claim to Polish provinces.

In May of 1942 Hull was still standing firm, and the Anglo-Soviet twenty-years treaty was signed in London without the recognition of Soviet pretensions to Polish territory. But this was the last stand. As the building up of pro-Soviet sentiment mushroomed in this country; as actual traitors and their dupes and allies crept into positions of greater influence in our government; as Stalin became deliberately more truculent and demanding, enabling his agents in the British government and in our government to capitalize on his implied threats to make a separate peace with

Hitler; and *as our lend-lease help to Russia and our own armed might both grew*, thus reducing Stalin's fears of Hitler: as these changes came there came a corresponding change in Stalin's attitude towards the Polish Government in London, towards the Polish "question," and towards a lot of other things with which we are not concerned here. And our own attitude of firmness melted away under these insidious pressures, right while the military strength to back up such firmness was steadily gaining stature.

In April, 1943, the Kremlin broke off diplomatic relations with the Polish Government In Exile on trumped-up grounds. Both the American and British Governments then became increasingly ready to sacrifice Polish territory in order to placate Stalin. By May, 1943, Roosevelt, Hopkins and their cohorts had already reached a decision to accept the Soviet stand that Poland's eastern boundaries must be changed. Sumner Welles for our government and Lord Halifax for the British government began urging on the Polish ambassador in Washington the necessity of concessions. At the Teheran Conference, in December, 1943, as came out much later, Roosevelt and Churchill agreed with Stalin to make the so-called Curzon Line the eastern boundary of Poland — in other words, to give all of Eastern Poland to Russia.

By some kind of diplomatic reasoning that is beyond the ken of us ordinary mortals, it was decided to salve the Churchill-Roosevelt consciences and compensate Poland for this lost territory by giving it a roughly equivalent amount of East Germany. For this purpose millions of Germans were to be expelled from land that had been German for centuries, and made refugees, while millions of Poles were to be put under the brutal power of the hostile Russian police state. All of this was decided without even consulting a single Pole, while Polish patriots were fighting heroically in the allied armies all over Europe, and the Polish underground army was keeping huge German forces immobilized in Poland.

71

Mr. Churchill took the lead in these particular "let's please Stalin" measures, because Mr. Roosevelt had a large Polish vote in this country and a fourth term to worry about. And right up through 1944 Roosevelt was consistently lying to Polish Prime Minister Mikolajczyk about American intentions, although he had long since assented to the Teheran arrangement. Churchill so declared in the British parliament, and confirmed the fact officially in a major conference.

On January 19, 1944, our government offered to act as mediator in restoring Soviet-Polish diplomatic relations. It was clear that acceptance of the territorial reshuffling agreed upon at Teheran was to be a basis for these discussions. But the Communists, in complete consistency with one of their most overworked and successful techniques, themselves rejected the offer. Having just barely won their point, thus knowing that the weak-kneed allies were willing to concede that much, they immediately held out for more. Their note of reply demanded that the Polish Government In Exile be reconstituted, to include Communist elements and to eliminate anti-Communist elements, before it could be considered fit to treat with representatives of the Kremlin.

All of this time, we know now, Stalin did not have the slightest intention of reaching any kind of accord with the Polish Government, or expectation of seeing it made over sufficiently to satisfy him. He had an entirely difference ace up his sleeve, and was just playing for time and confusion.

For the Polish Committee of National Liberation, later to be known diplomatically as the Provisional Government Of Poland and more realistically as The Lublin Gang, was taking shape. This committee of Stalin's stooges, including a leavening of renegade Poles, was put together in Moscow. As the Russian armies advanced, this committee set itself up in Lublin, on the eastern side of the Vistula. There followed the destruction of General Bor's Home Army by deception, as related above; and the later advance of the Russian armies into Warsaw and over the rest of Poland, as the Germans retreated. Concurrently with these events Mikolajczyk's government in London was left more and more deserted and unsupported by the British government and our own. On January 5, 1945, Stalin recognized the Lublin gang as the government of Poland and they established themselves in Warsaw. And then, in February, 1945, came the conference at Yalta.

At this conference Roosevelt and Churchill gave Stalin many countries which were not theirs to give, without even a word with or to the peoples of those countries who had fought as our allies in the war. Among them was Poland; almost half of it outright, as Russian territory, the remainder to be administered through a satellite government. They exacted the usual meaningless promises. The "Provisional Government" was to be broadened, to include other Polish leaders from Poland and abroad. And the new Polish Provisional Government of National Unity was to hold "free and unfettered" elections as soon as possible.

The commission set up to bring about the reorganization of the government included Molotov, and found itself completely stalled and stymied by him. Nobody could be taken into the government unless it met the approval and served the purposes of the Lublin gang. The gang remained, as it had begun, completely subservient to Stalin. Only Mikolajczyk and one or two lesser lights from the London group were taken into the government, in minor positions without power, as the best way ultimately to destroy them. Far from protesting, our government let Harry Hopkins assure Stalin that "we had no interest in seeing anyone connected with the present Polish Government in London involved in the new Provisional Government of Poland." And on July 5, 1945, the United States recognized this gang as the official government of Poland, appointed an ambassador to it, and withdrew all recognition of the Polish Government in

London. And several hundred Polish soldiers in Italy committed mass suicide rather than be returned to their country which had been betrayed.

As to the "free and unfettered" elections, that is a story needing many hundred pages. Despite the lack of any slightest support, moral or otherwise, from the western nations, the Poles did not give up easily. It took one of the most brutal, extensive, and ferret-like police state operations of all history two years to subdue them to the point where the Russians dared hold those elections which had been promised "as soon as possible." And some details indicating the extent to which they were "free and unfettered" still deserve a few brief paragraphs.

Almost immediately after Yalta sixteen prominent Polish underground leaders were enticed out of hiding, for consultation with Soviet officials, by the "word of honor" of a Russian Colonel as to their safe conduct and by the advice of the British government that they accept this assurance. They were promptly arrested and taken to Moscow for "trial." Molotov calmly announced these arrests at the conference for the organization of the United Nations in San Francisco, apparently as a way of telling us, and the Poles, and the world, how little Stalin was worried about British and American interference in Poland. And it was *after this* that Hopkins made his trip referred to above and we officially recognized the satellite government!

This was typical, on a very small scale, of the police-state measures used. Our very able and conscientious ambassador, Arthur Bliss Lane, strove in every sensible way he could — with our own State Department, from which he later resigned to tell the true story, as well as with the Warsaw government — to get some semblance of compliance with the Yalta promises. How much chance he had can perhaps best be indicated by the fact that when he finally gave up, and left, his home — the American embassy! — had been occupied and overrun by ten different native "squatters" whom the Warsaw government refused to let him evict; and there were over one hundred American citizens in Polish jails, none of whom the American ambassador had even been allowed to visit.

During the very period when these things were going on our State Department – or more specifically, Dean Acheson and Donald Hiss – insisted over Ambassador Lane's vigorous protest on making the Warsaw government that loan of ninety million dollars which I mentioned in my longer letter.

And during the very first of these two years under discussion UNRRA turned over to the Warsaw government, for distribution, as it saw fit, supplies worth four hundred and fifty million dollars, of which seventy-two percent was paid for by the United States.[13]

During these same two years violence and deportations and legalized murder and every police-state method were used, in a rising crescendo of volume and severity, as the time finally set for the elections approached. Since ninety percent of the Polish people are Catholic, and hence bitterly hostile to Communism even by religious training, it was necessary to eliminate, browbeat, and terrorize vast percentages of this population before it could be coerced into the straitjacket of the Communist tyranny.

The farce of the "free and unfettered" elections was held on January 19, 1947, almost two years after Yalta. Every known form of intimidation, suppression, and deception had been used against members of the Peasant Party, the only opposition to the government. They included murders by the police, beatings, torture, arrests, dismissals from jobs, expulsion from farms, expulsion from living quarters, wrecking of party premises, police prevention of meetings, police attacks on meetings, prevention of the use of printing facilities, the arrest of seventy-five of the candidates themselves, distribution of slanderous booklets in country sections by the army, threats against the children of voters, and a pre-election campaign by the police to make peasants sign pledge cards for the government slate. At the election itself it was made clear that any voter who did not casually let his vote be seen by the election officials was endangering his life or his family. Ambassador Lane reported all these things to Washington. Our State Department sent a note to Moscow that it was "especially perturbed" about them. Moscow made it clear that it was *not* perturbed about the American note. Ambassador Lane delivered notes of protest from our government to the Warsaw government itself, insisting that the solemn agreement of Yalta was being violated. The reply told Mr. Lane, in diplomatic jargon, to go peddle his papers and stop interfering with something that was none of his business. The elections were held, the government reported a practically unanimous victory, Ambassador Lane resigned, and the betrayal of Poland was finally complete.

III
NATION AFTER NATION
In China it was our ally Chiang Kai-shek whom we badgered, hamstrung, and abandoned; and tools of Stalin named Mao and Chou En-lai and Chu Teh whom we helped to take over Chiang's country. In Poland it had been our ally Mikolajczyk whom we deceived, abandoned, and disowned; and tools of Stalin with such names as Osubka-Morawski and Boleslaw Bierut whom we had helped to take over Mikolajczyk's country. In Yugoslavia it had been our ally Mihailovich whom we shamefully disowned, libelled, and allowed to be "legally" murdered for the Communists' propaganda purposes; and a tool of Stalin named Tito whom we helped to take over Mihailovich's country — for which Mihailovich had fought so hard and faithfully against our German enemies. In Albania and Bulgaria the characters of the drama were different but the plot remained the same. Essential parts

76

of the plot, as applicable, were used on other stages around the world. We cannot possibly review these plays scene by scene. Instead, let's simply catalogue their unhappy endings. In August, 1945, Stalin's troops occupied Southern Sakhalin and the Kurile Islands — thus pointing a permanent gun at Japan — by specific permission of the Yalta agreement. In October, 1945, Stalin's henchmen set up their "People's Republic" in Mongolia. In January, 1946, they proclaimed their "People's Republic" in Albania. In July, 1946, Stalin's mystery man, Tito, completed his crushing grasp of Yugoslavia by the public shooting of Mihailovich. In November, 1946, Stalin's agents took over Rumania and Bulgaria. In February, 1948, Stalin's lieutenants in Czecho-Slovakia pulled their coup d'état and formally placed that country behind the Iron Curtain. In May, 1948, Stalin's Asiatic servants set up their "People's Republic" in North Korea. In October, 1948, Stalin's troops took over Manchuria. By January, 1950, Stalin's viceroy, Mao, had completed his conquest of China. In October, 1950, Stalin's lackeys formalized their puppet state of East Germany. In May, 1951, Stalin's invaders seized Tibet. Whether Iran or Indo-China or Greece or Formosa is next we do not know. We know only that the policy of "containment of Communism," which has been the theoretical key to our course these recent years, contains *nothing* except a cover-up for our ignominy and folly.

For in all of the sociological equations that Stalin has solved in order to make these various conquests, there has been one dependable factor. This has been the moral support and the financial support of our government, however cleverly disguised, and however skillfully the facts have been kept from the American people. David Martin points out that in 1941 Stalin was able to "sell" Tito to the United States largely because "the State Department and the Office of War Information contained personnel whose sympathy the Communists could count upon in advance." This situation has remained true and grown steadily worse in the decade since. Communists and their sympathizers, beguiling many innocents into mouthing their propaganda for them, are causing us right now to fight the most idiotic war in all history. In this war with Communist China, in which we have already suffered more than a hundred thousand casualties, our Seventh Fleet is today under orders to protect the coastline of our enemy Mao for him, from any possible attack by our friend and ally, Chiang Kai-shek. And six hundred thousand trained and patriotic Chinese soldiers on Formosa are refused their request to fight with us and for us, while our sons are being killed in battle and murdered as prisoners of war behind the lines. These and so many other facts show the truth, through all the cloud of sophistry put out by the State Department.

The original "angels" for the promotion of Stalin's post-war imperialism were Roosevelt and Churchill. By 1946 Churchill had awakened, and publicly confessed, to the folly of the course he had pursued. By 1948 he was proclaiming that "we lie in the grip of even worse perils than those we have surmounted." And the evidence is strong that in the closing weeks of his life even Roosevelt came to realize that he had been horribly duped. But by 1946 Roosevelt was dead and Churchill was out of power. The British socialists, partly through an ideological kinship with theoretical communism, and partly through an infiltration of actual Communists probably greater even than in our government, were easily led by the nose down whatever paths Stalin chose to take them. And President Truman, from the hour he took office, has been sucked steadily deeper into the quicksand of pro-Communist influence, until today he is virtually a captive of its pressures. How willing a captive he may be, because of his desire for the clever, insidious, and — in the past — amazingly effective political support of the extreme Left Wing, is a question of interpretation more than of facts.

But of the facts to prove Truman's captivity there can be no doubt. His dismissal of MacArthur and the manner of that dismissal; his support of "Point Four" (a Communist scheme copied almost verbatim from a Communist blueprint, and already "sold" to many gullible American innocents); his unswerving attempts to block or hamstring every investigation into Communist infiltration of our government agencies; his acquiescence in the State Department policy; his maintenance within his White House family, and appointment or attempted appointment to various government jobs, of persons with known pro-Communist sympathies; his humiliating acceptance of the fraudulent arrest of American citizens and the insulting treatment of our official representatives in all parts of the Communist world; his refusal to follow the urging of MacKenzie King and do something about the spy ring which was right then stealing our atomic secrets; his suppression of the Wedemeyer Report on China; his contradictory attitudes towards Franco and Tito; his readiness to debase our currency and to spend us into bankruptcy; these are all but details, of which there are hundreds more. The real facts merge into just one huge and simple fact, the actual and astounding progress, recorded above, which Communism has made since Truman became President in 1945 — and which is steadily gaining greater world-wide momentum.

That there are more Communists and Communist sympathizers in our government today than ever before seems to me almost a certainty. That some of them are men of great standing, in high places, and least suspected, is at least a frightening possibility. And I see no possible chance of weeding them out, or of learning one-half the truth, so long as Truman remains in power and his attitude of high-handed obstruction remains as their chief bulwark of defense. Even the great furore which has now been raised, over the colossal corruption in our government, has served the Communists well. It has taken the heat off the far more dangerous permeation of treason throughout that same government — and may even have been started and encouraged by Communists behind the scenes for that purpose.

Let me make it crystal clear that I do not think Harry Truman is a Communist or a sympathizer with Russian imperial ambitions. He is, I do think, a callous politician, with few scruples about the means used to achieve a political end. But I am sure that deep inside, and fundamentally, he is a loyal and patriotic American. I only wish that my pen had the inspired power to make Truman himself see, through the maze that has been pulled over his eyes, the imminence, the immensity, and the horror of the Communist threat in its stark reality.

It is far too much to expect. For the real trouble is a callousness throughout the whole mood and the collective conscience of the American people. How can we expect either Roosevelt or Truman to have been disturbed by the barbarous Katyn Massacre, or to have reduced for that reason their pampering appeasement and generosity to its perpetrators? The news of a similar mass murder, of eight thousand of our own sons and brothers, as prisoners of war behind the Korean lines, caused only a temporary ripple of indignation across the national consciousness; and we go serenely on negotiating with, and making new concessions to, the cold-blooded murderers.

What's the matter with us, anyway? Neither facts nor pictures seem to sink into our centers of feeling any more. They remain just words and lines and forms, objective phenomena outside the glazed surface of our noumenal existence. The physical suffering, the mental anguish, the never-ceasing terror of our fellow human beings, represented by these words and pictures, no longer reach through the glaze to activate our imaginations or to excite our sympathies.

The lowest estimate any recognized authority is willing to

make places the number of slave laborers in Russia at eight million persons. It may be twice that great. Most of these people have been brutally torn from their homes and their families somewhere, for the very reason that they loved their homes and families; that they were not the kind of people who could be expected to sacrifice civilized loyalties to the service of a Communist tyranny. Very few have ever escaped from these camps, and reached an opportunity to tell the West about them. But some have, and enough for the purpose. There are available carefully restrained, documented, and incontrovertible expositions of the conditions of brutality, filth, disease, terror, and hopelessness under which these victims — men like you and me — work out the days or years until they are no longer worth famine-rations to their captors. This knowledge has been available throughout all the years that our government has been helping to hand ever more peoples and provinces to "good old Uncle Joe." It is available to all those Communists and their sympathizers in our midst who befoul our schools, our public forums, and even our courts, with their rantings about idealism and freedom. We read about these things in the newspapers for a cursory minute, and then turn with a shrug to the sports pages or the comics.

America was long looked to as the light of the world; a land and a people of happiness and strength; a nation that had for itself, and promoted for others wherever its influence reached, justice and honor and decency and freedom. The remembrance of that light dies slowly, even when it can no longer be seen. Today in Poland, in China, in Czecho-Slovakia, in numberless areas behind the Iron Curtain, there are millions of families — like yours and mine — which have been decimated, starved, and frightened into abject submission; but which still cling to the dream that presently, maybe even next week or next year, the United States is going to come, in all its beneficent majesty, to rescue them from the inhuman tyranny which owns them now. In their moments of greatest misery or despair they ask the question: "When will the Americans come?" The Americans, unfortunately, all of us, are busy playing our little games; while our government, far from worrying about how the Iron Curtain might ever be lifted, is frequently lending a hand — as to Mao in China — to those who are trying to bring down another section of the curtain to swallow up another piece of the globe.

There are good diplomats and bad diplomats, of course. But above all there are too many diplomats, and they have too much power. They sit around their conference tables omnipotently giving away the lives and homes and souls of millions of people who are helpless in the shuffle. Fourteen million Germans were ruthlessly uprooted, and scattered as refugees over the face of central Europe. Two million of them died, of disease or starvation. The remaining twelve million are still refugees, adding their own destitution to a precarious German economy, and creating ever new problems for the diplomats to confer about importantly at their stuffed-shirt meetings. And was this atrocity committed in order to punish these Germans for having supported Hitler? Not at all, for the people of East Poland fought Hitler as long and as hard as anybody else in Europe, and they were treated just as horribly, in the same package deal. This piece of barbarism on the epic scale was arranged simply to please Stalin. It fitted into his plans. Who protested? Or who really cared, in America or anywhere else — except among the victims? Fourteen million people, two million of them dead — just so many words, or sounds! The suffering of fourteen million individual human beings just didn't register with us, unless you or I were one of the fourteen million.

As we sit in our warm homes, after a happy meal with our families, and turn on our television sets or radios, it is hard for us to think of a man just like ourselves always half-starved, always half-frozen, haggard and hopeless, re-membering the days when he too was free, as he is brutally driven to finish up the literal exhaustion of his body in labor for the benefit of the very tyrant who has enslaved him. It is harder still to remember that there are *millions* of such men; or that in the past six years, *six hundred millions* of our fellow human beings have been placed under the merciless heel of this monster and the bestial control of his henchmen and police.

For the pusillanimous part that we have played in all this spreading horror; for our indifference to the grief of others; for our apathy to the crimes we saw and our blindness to those we should have seen; for our gullibility in the acceptance of veneered treason and our easy forgetfulness even when the veneer had been rubbed off; for all our witting and unwitting help to the vicious savages of the Kremlin and to their subordinate savages everywhere, may God — and our fellow men — some day forgive us!

IV
HOW SAFE ARE WE?

We can never earn the forgiveness of these people we have betrayed, however, by inspiration, help, or leadership to throw off their chains of tyranny, if we ourselves are first shackled by the same tyrant. And no man, outside of the innermost councils of the Kremlin, can judge the closeness or the extent of our danger. I can only put down, for our readers to evaluate as they wish, those facts, conjectures, and opinions which worry me most as portents of the coming storm.

1. To my mind Korea remains — what it has been from the very beginning — primarily a practice field on which Stalin holds his rehearsal for the war to come. Even the blindest partisan of Acheson and Marshall must admit that Stalin has been able, by the levers of diplomacy, to adjust

both the expanse and nature of the Korean conflict at will. Today, with ground action held to a minimum by going through the endless motions of fraudulent truce talks, Stalin is using the practice field for his jets. Drew Pearson, in his column of February 15, said: "The blunt fact is that the Kremlin is using Korea as a graduate school to train Russian pilots how to fly against American planes." It is now almost a year since I prophesied this development in speeches from notes which were later converted into the body of this pamphlet. And I pointed out that as to ground fighting the rehearsal was already far advanced. Since that time I have seen only confirmation of my worry that, as the Spanish Civil War was provoked by Stalin to be a training ground for World War II, the Korean Civil War has been deliberately planned to serve the same purpose for World War III.

2. Despite all the "important" meetings and publicized diplomatic victories and ballyhoo and clamor, I am very much afraid we are getting absolutely no place in Europe. England couldn't help us if it wanted to, because over the past twenty years appeasement has become a too deeply ingrained principle of British foreign policy for any government to stand up against that policy until the very day of attack. France has nothing to help with, except troubles to add to the confusion. Germany has no will to become the battleground on which the armies of the East and West would meet. In Italy there are undoubtedly more Communists today than there are in Russian-controlled Poland. In Belgium we sided with the Communists in depriving the people of their beloved king – despite his impressive victory at the polls, which we flouted – and we now ask those same people to accept privations to help us fight the Communists. In Europe the governments think we are suckers, the people think we are meddlesome fools. For years our State Department has been giving ample reasons for both opinions. All we are actually accomplishing in Europe is the waste of a

tremendous amount of American money, one more excuse for the strangling regimentation of our economy, and a false confidence in the American people of an approach towards greater security. Stalin could not have planned the whole thing better himself — as maybe he did.

3. We are following so exactly, and now at so obviously an accelerated pace, the precise course, of spending ourselves towards bankruptcy, of indecision and confusion, of weak-kneed ineffectiveness and humiliating appeasement, which has been laid out for us in the Communist prospectus. And the same clique which has brought us to this pass, still in control, still has no clear aim to offer, of war or of peace or of negotiation, to our enemy or to ourselves. All is confusion; and it becomes daily more inconceivable that it is not brilliantly arranged confusion, rapidly reaching a climax.

4. We are swallowing the Tito bait, hook, line, and sinker. Which means that we are pouring huge quantities of war matériel and of our newest armament into the hands of the Communists to be used against us.

I am aware that few of our readers will believe me, for the deception has been too cleverly planned and too realistically executed. I have no proof; how could I? But I have the right to state my opinion, so long as it is clearly labeled opinion, nevertheless. What's more, I have a solemn duty to state that opinion, under the circumstances, and to set forth the evidence that supports it.

I should have liked to have given the story of the betrayal of Mihailovich, as a background for these paragraphs. There wasn't room or time, for no brief summary could have given the essence of that story as in the case of Poland. Because Tito is a far cleverer man than Osubka-Morawski, or even Molotov, it takes a huge and cumulative mass of details to construct the truth of the Yugoslavian horror.

Suffice it to say here that when Josip Broz Tito was sprung on the world, in July, 1942, by a new clandestine radio station calling itself "Radio Free Yugoslavia," nobody knew who he was or where he came from, nor even if Tito was his right name. They still do not, to this day. It has been claimed that he was a Croatian, but there was no documentation and no convincing evidence. All that did become clear was that he was an agent of Stalin, obviously well trained in Russia, who had been sent into Yugoslavia to take victory out of the hands of our allies who were doing the fighting, as Mao did in China and the Lublin gang in Poland. By promoting civil strife while the energies of real patriots were needed to fight the German conquerors, by lies about Mihailovich more foul and more ably spread abroad than those of Mao about Chiang, by a rising terrorism as ruthless as that of Mao, by the full support of arms and advisors and money from Russia, by the falsification of allied military intelligence, by the growing support of America and Britain obtained through Russian pressures and Stalin's sympathizers within those countries, and by resort to every Communist technique from treason to mass murder, he succeeded. In July, 1946, he became the undisputed and allpowerful dictator of Yugoslavia. He remains so to this day.

The myth that Mao was an "agrarian reformer," or that even if a Communist he was an independent and nationalistic Communist who might be persuaded to break with Stalin, was the most carefully built up lie of all the pro-Chinese Communist propaganda. The best-known biography of Mao, written by a little English pink now residing in this country, followed this Communist line so closely as to omit all mention of Mao's ever having been in Moscow, although it purported to give full and voluminous details about his whole life. The plain well-established facts are that Mao was not only trained in Moscow, but was considered such a brilliant pupil as to have been used to teach other Communists – in Moscow – his methods. But the myth was persistently and persuasively enough presented for it to serve as a partial justification of our support of Mao for years.

To anybody who looked at the fundamentals of the situation, and ignored the smokescreen tossed up around them, that myth was ridiculous. But it served its purpose — a temporary one — very well. To anybody who looks at the fundamentals, and ignores the red herrings that have been so cleverly dragged across the trail, the myth that Tito has ever really broken with Stalin is just as ridiculous. But this lie was intended to serve a much deeper and longer-range purpose. It had to be much more realistically and convincingly staged. The stakes were enormous. And you could almost hear Stalin saying to Tito, as one wrestler would say to a "fixed" opponent, "now remember, you've got to make it good." They made it good. And the fiction of Tito's rebellion has served some wonderful propaganda purposes for the Communists, as simply a dividend on their investment for the real capital returns. Could you imagine an any more beautiful set-up, or one more in keeping with the deep cunning of Stalin's nature?

"But look at all the terrible things Stalin and Tito have said about each other, and all the bitterness they have inculcated in their respective subjects towards each other," somebody says. "How could they undo this cleavage even if they wanted to?" To which I reply "Horseradish!" This name-calling and this propaganda has been peanuts compared to that used by Stalin and Hitler towards each other for years; and their respective subjects were even given a deep-rooted ideological base for their mutual bitterness. But when the time came Stalin and Hitler could pull those subjects together as friends and collaborators, or set them at each other's throats as mortal enemies, at the turn of a phrase and the drop of a whispered command. The same procedure is infinitely easier as between Tito and Stalin.

It is a well recognized principle of Communist technique that "where there is sufficient strength, there can be a show of weakness." But where there is a real weakness there must always be a show of strength, and the weakness must never be exposed. Does anybody think that if Stalin did not really own Tito, and that if this fact were not known to the really top Communists, this festering sore of rebellion and this flaunting of organizational weakness — in the tightest hierarchy of power the world has ever seen — would be allowed to exist for years? That Stalin, who could have his closest working companions liquidated in the "purge" trials, for the sake of eliminating any question of his own absolute power; or who could reach all the way into Mexico, through the careful defenses of a trained and suspicious revolutionary, to have Trotsky assassinated, to show that not even a doctrinal schism could be tolerated; that this man would have been unwilling or unable to wipe out Tito in a week if Tito threatened in the slightest his completely autocratic and imperial command? Not one place in the world can you find where Stalin has lost the slightest degree of prestige or of authority with his Communist subordinates, due to Tito's alleged revolt — because they all know better.

There are other glaring giveaways to this gigantic fraud, for anybody who cares to look with both eyes open. One is the persistency with which we are told, frequently as though the information has been obtained by some vigilant intelligence service of our government, and usually by people known in the past as Communist sympathizers but now supposedly reformed, that Stalin is about to attack Yugoslavia. There really were plenty of reliable intelligence reports that the North Korean Communists were about to cross the 38th Parallel in force, but these were kept from the American people and even from MacArthur. We never heard any rumors of Stalin's intentions with regard to Tibet until the country had already been seized. But we drink our coffee every other morning to the accompaniment of planted newspaper predictions that Stalin is about to go after Tito at last and we had better send more supplies to this first line of our defense. Just how gullible can we become?

And the last revealing reaction I shall mention, before resting my case, is the one that causes me to number this acceptance of Tito among the darkest clouds on the horizon. For our government is loaded with people who, to put it diplomatically, had a recognizable "soft" attitude towards Stalin for a long time. Many of them have now been forced, by a rising doubt and anger in the American people, or have found it expedient, to take a public position of "realistic hardness." They go loudly for an almost fantastic preparedness and rearmament program, with a great deal more emphasis on how many billions we spend than on what we get for our money. They are all for arming and "coordinating" our allies, whether we have adequate equipment for our own forces or not. And *the* "ally," the bulwark against Stalinism, the man we must arm and help with money and materials above all other, is Tito. Franco, who has actually fought for his life and the life of his nation against Stalin's murderous agents, we mustn't help or depend on, because he is not democratic! The newspapers report Truman and Eisenhower as making gratuitously insulting remarks about Franco, right at the very time our government is supposedly exerting its best efforts to arrange for our establishment of air bases in Spain. But Tito, well we mustn't look a gift horse in the mouth, or be squeamish about allies when we need them so badly. Pour in the guns and the butter, too, in mammoth quantities and with never-resting speed, before Stalin attacks. And pouring them in we are; in such staggering amounts that the State Department would not dare tell the truth to the American people, and any figures they did publish could no more be believed than the calculated reverse lies they told about our aid to Chiang Kai-shek or to the Republic of South Korea. (If you think this language is harsh, instead of merely factual, look up the records and study the Congressional hearings for yourself.)

5. We are so rapidly losing prestige everywhere in the

world, the diplomatic tide is turning so strongly against us, the number of votes against us at times and of *voters* against us at all times in the U.N. deliberations is so alarmingly increasing, that even our pretense of anti-Communist leadership is about to be lost for the lack of a following. And unless a miracle can be worked, in awakening the American people to an angry and determined stand, Communist China will presently be seated in the United Nations with the blessings of our "allies" England and France. We are giving our strength more and more to others as we approach closer and closer to being left alone.

6. Our own government is literally falling apart at the seams. There not only is neither truth, nor honesty, nor honor to be found in its decrees or in its actions; they are no longer even expected, and their absence is brazenly taken for granted. There is no charted course to which our people subscribe, no goals towards which we might confidently aim, no leadership that either leads or has any sense of direction. As a whole, or in its separate departments and bureaus, our government is at an all-time low; in efficiency, in economy, in integrity, in clarity of purpose, in the calibre and character of its top personnel, and in the respect and regard accorded it by the American people. And the very processes of our constitutional procedure make it inevitable that this deterioration, disintegration, and discord will become far worse, and weaken our dissipated national effectiveness far more, between now and next January.

That corruption permeates every pore of the monstrosity of organization and disorganization to which our bureaucracy has expanded is known and tolerated. That every gesture of the administration towards investigation of either corruption or treason will be a whitewash is accepted with cynical acquiescence by a legislative majority which cannot itself show all clean hands. We have men appointed to ambassadorships or important departmental posts whose chief qualifications are that they need to get out of the country, or that nobody can prove they are actual Communists. And the government is falling apart, not because of external pressures of an aroused citizenry, but because the very foulness inside is too great to permit connecting sinews of strength and of command.

The administration flouts both our constitution and the best-known laws on our legislative books. Its arbitrary choosing of the congressional enactments which it wishes to ignore and of those which it cares to enforce has already brought us from a government of laws to a government of corrupt little men. During the next several months these corrupt little men will quarrel still more among themselves; and even our soundest citizens outside the government will be split by bitterness within our political divisions and subdivisions. To what extent these enormous elements of at least temporary weakness have been contrived and fomented by the Communists there is no way of knowing. But that the Kremlin is far better informed as to our situation than are the majority of our own citizens you can be sure. And that a badly leaking ship, with a crooked and inefficient crew and a broken rudder, is an invitation to ruthless and well-armed brigands watching their opportunity — that is a known fact which makes our present circumstances the most alarming in our history.

7. The last worry about the outlook, which I shall mention here, is the growing quiet before the storm. It seemed to me a year ago that I could sense a tendency, on the part of the Kremlin, to a greater appearance of reasonableness; that tensions were being maneuvered into a soothing semblance of static equilibrium; that we were going to be led into feeling that our rearmament program, our going through motions in Europe, our delicately balanced stalemate in Korea, our grimaces about lines that must not be crossed, were causing hesitation in Moscow and warranted

91

optimism in Washington. We would begin to hear a great deal of inside revelations about Russia's lack of oil, and disagreements within the Politburo, and disaffection among the satellite nations, and possible breaks between Mao and Stalin, and "rust holes in the Iron Curtain." The impression would be nurtured that time was on our side; that having at last made proper plans we could just watch while those plans gradually advanced us to an unassailable position; that we could relax in the meantime, and start jousting with ourselves over some such issue as corruption in our government. It seems to me today that the feeling of a year ago has been borne out by events. Again I hope that my interpretation is as wrong as my fears are great.

There are other reasons for worry, especially connected with a time schedule which, I am terribly afraid, can be projected like a curve from an adequate number of known points. But I have been far too much of an alarmist already.

V
THE TIME IS NOW

It was Thursday night, Mr. Regnery, when you called me on the telephone. It was Friday night before I had a chance to start on this "postscript" which I am going to deliver to you in New York next Thursday. Because of the time pressure I have written it, in the purple-passage language of a less cynical age, "at white heat." I do not even know whether you will be willing to publish this new material, or whether we can squeeze it within the pages planned and the costs required by your quotation to distributors of the pamphlet. But I had to write it — now.

In this letter, as in the earlier one, I make no pretense to either originality or scholarship. You have already recognized, I am sure, that my story of the Communist treatment of Poland is primarily a condensation of just one chapter in William Henry Chamberlin's great book, *America's Second*

92

Crusade. My background knowledge for the condensation came from Arthur Bliss Lane's *I Saw Poland Betrayed.* All the rest of the letter, except where clearly shown to be a transcript of my own thoughts, is merely history lifted piecemeal from newspaper and magazine reports or from the pages of honest historians. I have had no contact with so-called "original sources."

My purpose in writing this letter I hope is plain. I want to alert as many of my fellow-Americans as the pamphlet or book can reach to the dangerous difference between appearances and reality, in our fight against Communism and in the progress of that fight. I have given the best I had to this effort, however inadequate it may be. This statement is made in frankness and humility, for a sound reason. I want to ask the reader who has had the patience to come with me this far to do me a favor in return.

You — such reader — may not be convinced. The best that I had may not have been good enough. But you are a patriotic American who would like to know, and would be willing to face, the truth. At the end of this letter there is a list of books.[18] In each case the name of the author, the title of the book, and the publisher is given. Many of them are books which the Communists have tried very hard, and in most cases successfully, to keep out of your hands. For this purpose the Communists have infiltrated and dominated the book-review pages of many of our great periodicals; they have planted clerks in many book stores to hide "hostile" books under the counters or to steer purchasers away from such books; they have influenced library purchasing and have intimidated publishers. These are provable and proven facts. As a result many of these books — in fact most of them — are out of print and may be hard to obtain, even just to read and not to own. It took me four months of diligent effort to find a copy of Arthur Bliss Lane's *I Saw Poland Betrayed* that I could even borrow; it took the best secondhand book dealers in Boston five months to find one that I could buy.

But to know the truth, especially important truth that has been deliberately hidden from you, is worth some labor. Get hold of these books, especially the ones that I have starred. Read them for yourself, with an open and unbiased mind. Take nothing for granted, from me or from anybody else. Judge the dependability of the books, the veracity of their authors, the importance of their message, entirely on your own. When you finish far less than half of the list you will be satisfied, I believe with all my head and heart, that the truth is far more shocking and the danger far more horrible than I have been able to paint them here.

When you know the truth, then what? What is to be done? That question is being asked, at least silently, by literally millions of people who have never heard of me or my small efforts. For those who care about my answers, I have two. They are honest and direct.

The first is, weigh and appraise all news items against this larger background of truth. For the game goes on, without recess or change. A few years ago there was a conference at San Francisco to set up the United Nations. It was proclaimed as a great step forward – for us, for everybody. We know now that the conference was brilliantly stage-managed and disastrously "loaded" against the best interests of our country – by Alger Hiss and his allies. A few months ago there was another conference at San Francisco, to sign formally our peace treaty with Japan. It was proclaimed as a great step forward – for us, and for the free world. The actual treaty written by Dulles may have been a conscientious and superb piece of work. But in my opinion it will take far less than five years, if we are all around that long, to show that the appearances of this conference were just as deceptive, the stage-management just as phony, and the set-up just as "loaded" against America's best interests – by a man who refuses to turn his back on Alger Hiss, and *his* allies. Certainly there are few things the Kremlin wanted more than for us to put Japan on its own, so that they could go to work on that country without our on-the-spot supervision. And it is already known that the Soviet did not even have any intention of opposing the treaty until the last minute, when it seemed wise to do so for their usual purposes of deception.

A few years ago we set out to win friends and rehabilitate nations through UNRRA. We know now that the UNRRA supplies for Poland were channeled through the Communist Menshikov, and used to strengthen and win friends for the Communist government; that the UNRRA supplies for China were largely channeled through Madame Sun Yat-sen, and used to strengthen and win friends for Mao's Communists; and that the same pattern was widely followed elsewhere. Then came the "Marshall Plan," originally designed to apply equally to the Soviet "republics" and their satellites, as to other nations. It is a little early to prove that the chief result of the Marshall Plan, even as used, was to strengthen the hand of socialist governments, permeated through and through by Communist sympathizers, who were playing footsie-wootsie with the Soviets far more cozily than was ever dreamed of by most of their citizens — or ours. But the facts are all there. Just where are all those staunch friends the Marshall Plan was supposed to have won for us, in our fight against the Communists? Even England, which has claimed to be by far the most appreciative of its beneficiaries, is consistently on the side of Mao and the Chinese Communists, against ourselves. And if Churchill really tries to reverse this tacit working arrangement, he knows that he will be thrown out of power.

Now it is NATO. General Eisenhower may be doing his utmost to have it make sense, and serve our needs. But I, for one, have persistent fears that five years from now — again if we are all around that long — it may prove to have been just as phony, and just as futile or worse, as were UNRRA and the Marshall Plan. There is a difference, however. With UNRRA we were spending hundreds of millions of dollars. With the Marshall Plan we were spending billions. With NATO we are spending tens of billions. It has just recently been announced that we should raise our sights, as to the costs of a greatly expanded NATO program, to three times their present level. We shall be talking about *hundreds of billions* to "contain" Communism in Europe before long. [The goal set at Lisbon for NATO, as announced since this was written, was an army to cost *three hundred billion dollars!*][17]

The lesser grist of news in the day's mill is all of the same crop. Dean Acheson has just reversed the finding of his own State Department loyalty board, in order to "clear" Oliver E. Clubb — referred to on Page 50 above — by personal decree. (It is hard to believe that Mr. Acheson had read the eighty-seven pages of testimony recorded from Clubb's appearance before the House Un-American Activities Committee.) Mr. John Paton Davies Jr., whose "suspension" we also recorded on Page 50, is now right-hand advisor to Commissioner McCloy in Germany, helping to determine our policies with regard to the German government and the German people. Russia has just stolen our "fabulously effective" secret mine, reported to be completely undetectable by ships which it endangers; the newspapers give the matter headlines for one day, and nobody pays any more attention. The repeated testimony of many witnesses before the McCarran Commmittee has now identified forty-seven persons connected with the Institute of Pacific Relations as having been Communists or Soviet agents. Letters and memoranda from the files of the IPR, found hidden in Edward C. Carter's barn in Lee, Massachusetts, show that the IPR was busily disseminating Communist propaganda during its period of activity discussed in the pages above. (But you will have to wait a long time before you find those details in some of our newspapers.)

"Dr." Owen Lattimore, now before the Committee, is daily admitting "errors" in his previous testimony under oath. Kiplinger writes that the truce talks in Korea are about to end but — with the appearance of surprise — that we are not going to "give" Formosa to the Reds as one of our concessions after all! Newspaper reports make clear that the Chinese Communists have used the "truce" period, exactly as they used those forced on Chiang Kai-shek by General Marshall, to build up their forces, so that they now have overwhelming superiority of numbers in the air as well as on the ground. The amount of waste, increasingly revealed, that we are buying instead of armament with our defense billions makes us shudder over the extent to which this waste may be deliberate and intentional. And I have just heard a Pulitzer Prize-winning former editor, a great "liberal," tell our local Chamber of Commerce that the logic of events in Asia is with Mao and his Communists so that he will become the ally of ourselves instead of Stalin! Truly, the more it all changes the more it is just the same thing; and the more I bring this letter up to date, the more I am just repeating what I have already written. I wish simply to underscore my first answer: Read the news with a penetrating glance for the broad sweep of terrifying truth between the lines.[18]

My second answer is plainer yet. Make your voice heard and your vote felt. Write letters, make telephone calls, personally speak your sentiments — to newspaper and magazine editors, to senators and congressmen and local representatives, to teachers and preachers and just plain friends. Use judgment in order to be fair, restraint in order to be effective, but persistence in order to be heard. And don't let up. The Communists *never* let up.[19]

Make your voice heard and your vote felt. Our enemies are neither Democrats nor Republicans. Our enemies are the

Communists. Our opponents are their allies, their dupes, and those who support them for whatever cause. This is a *fundamental* fight which must not be stymied by partisanship. Martin Dies, to whose pioneering efforts at uncovering Communist traitors in our midst this country may owe its very existence, was a Democrat. Senator McCarran, who is continuing the same undertaking so doggedly today, is a Democrat. Senator Nixon and Congressman Judd are Republicans. The whole effort rises and must rise above the level of ordinary political considerations. But it is high time for us to start guiding our feet by the lamp of long experience. It is time for us to put in charge of our government men — and only those men — whom we know everything about; concerning whom there can be no possible question as to their intellectual honesty, their abilities, their own patriotism, or the patriotism of those with whom they have been closely associated. It is high time that, by impeachment or by elections, we stop "trusting the future to those who have betrayed the past."

Sincerely,

ROBERT H. W. WELCH, JR.

Notes

1. Browder hung on, as Communist liaison agent in the International Settlement at Shanghai, for several months yet. He then went first to Moscow, from which he was sent back to America in 1929 to take over the American Communist Party.

2. Stalin had actually won his point, that in non-industrialized countries such as China the orthodox approach to Communism, through agitation among the urban proletariat, was to be superseded by the opportunism of "agrarian reform" among the peasants, by August, 1928. And Mao was, of course, one of the leaders of the fighting remnants of Communists which had fled first to Hunan Province after the debacle at Hankow, and which in 1928 was holding on in the mountains of Kiangsi. But it was not till 1929 (when Trotsky was finally banished from Russia) that Stalin's completely autocratic power in international communism became undeniable, or that the entirely new pattern for the Communist conquest of China began to emerge out of the wreckage of the old one.

3. It is actually less than a thousand miles from the mountains of Kiangsi to the city of Yenan. Because these Communist holdouts were constantly on the run before Chiang's troops and because they had to live on the land as marauding brigands, the main body of these forces traveled between five and six thousand circuitous miles in order to make this passage. And the Communists have done their utmost to give the migration of this murdering rabble an epic flavor by eulogizing it as the "Long March." There has even been one attempt to appeal to the heartstrings of the world by a book glorifying the "Children of the Long March."

4. This treaty, originally signed on April 13, 1941, had stated as one of its three main points that it was to be valid for five years. Naturally, Soviet and Japanese diplomats did not get together, after Pearl Harbor, with a coterie of reporters and photographers, to announce solemnly to the world that the pact still held. But they did make it clear to each

other, by notes and by actions, that both governments considered the treaty not to have been affected by America's entry into the war as the enemy of one and the ally of the other. And Russia's withdrawal of some of her forces from the Manchurian border, on the basis of this agreement, made it easier for Japan to score victories against ourselves during 1942.

5. When the question is one of census, either military or civilian, in China, there is always room for dispute. It is definitely known, however, that by the *middle* of 1945, Mao had at least five hundred thousand men in organized military ranks, and that the number mushroomed very rapidly during the remainder of the year. The figure I have given for the end of 1945 is an estimate based on the consensus of information available. Rifles and training for these troops was a different matter. The rifles and ammunition were to come from the Japanese stockpile in Manchuria. Time required for the arming, training, and grouping of these troops was to be supplied by the consecutive truces forced on Chiang Kai-shek by General George C. Marshall.

6. The same considerations as to problems of census apply here as in Note 5. One authority, for whose opinion I have very high respect, says that the number of inhabitants in that part of Shensi Province controlled by Mao in 1937 could have been as high as 1,500,000. This would of course, have represented roughly 1/3 of 1% instead of 1/8 of 1%, of the population of China. The only absolutely positive conclusion for the reader, therefore, is that the figure lies somewhere between these limits. But the numbers I have given represent my own best summation of the evidence.

7. See Note 9.

8. Since this was written, she has refused to tell the McCarran Committee whether or not she was a member of the Communist Party, on the grounds of self-incrimination.

9. As is made clear in the parenthetical comment following this statement, about one-half of this number were administrators, technicians, traders — and their families — and all the other adjuncts to a huge occupation of enemy territory for imperialistic purposes. That they were all a part of the *forces* of that occupation is made clear by the fact that the whole three million were repatriated when Japan lost the war.

10. On the first printing of *May God Forgive Us,* this statement was picked up as being erroneous, on the grounds that "September, 1945" should have read "November, 1945." The critic was himself confused

by the fact that General Hurley did *resign* in November. But there is in my possession a copy of a letter sent me by General Hurley in which he himself has stated, correctly: "I left China on September 22, 1945, and have never returned."

11. The Communists boasted loudly, "Well, we got Grew"; and took to themselves noisy credit for the conquest. It has also been widely argued that Acheson, although out of the State Department at the time, had a strong hand in the actual ouster of Grew. But Grew himself feels otherwise, and I have written this paragraph in accordance with the interpretation of events which he himself has given me. The point at issue makes no difference in the real developments, which were the substitution for Grew's attitude of skepticism, about Communist activities and intentions, of the Acheson policy of pro-Soviet "understanding" and collaboration.

12. This refusal of recognition of Poland's 1939 boundaries was accomplished, with typical Communist indirection, not by what was said but by what was omitted. In this pact the Soviet Government "recognized that the Soviet-German treaties of 1939 dealing with territorial changes in Poland had lost their validity." But there was no Soviet acceptance of the previous boundaries which the Stalin-Hitler partnership had wiped out. And this was not because the point was *overlooked*, for Sikorski did everything he could to get such actual recognition of Poland's territorial integrity, and it was *because of this omission* that several members of his cabinet resigned.

13. The remaining twenty-eight percent was paid by countries to which we were making "loans," almost entirely out of those loans.

14. For a reprinting of this book, more than three years after this paragraph was written, it would be easiest simply to put a note here saying that obviously the evidence was not valid and my fears were unfounded. But that would be too easy, for I don't think it would be true.

The long-range patience of the Communist leaders and the planned gradualism of the Communist advance are both undeniable. But Stalin was willing to destroy any friend, distort or discard any Communist doctrine, alter or reverse any Communist strategy, for the sake of increasing his own personal power. I believe that his obsession with the desire to rule the world might easily have caused him to have taken the gamble of atomic attack and all-out war on the United States, if he had still had sufficient energy, health and life expectancy left by the time he himself thought the gamble offered some chance of success. I think there is considerable evidence that the fall of 1952 had been tentatively

101

set as a time for such an attack, and that we may well have been saved from the beginning of the "hottest" war the planet has so far known, at that time, by Stalin's realistic appraisal of his own health. This is basically a conjecture, of course, but I am not willing to admit that the conjecture has, or had, no palpable foundations.

Additional Notes For The January, 1960 Edition

15. Whether this would have been true if Stalin had lived there is no way of knowing. But the Communist conspiratorial apparatus in Iran, which was exposed and exploded in the fall of 1954, was the most powerful, in relation to the size of the nation involved, that has ever been fully revealed *before* it was successful in taking over a country. So de Courcy, who is of course the "private intelligence agency" referred to, could have been entirely right if Stalin's death had not caused the reins to get tangled.

Also, it is possible that de Courcy was correct, and even reasonably accurate, that Stalin had been stockpiling four atom bombs per month. But not bombs of Soviet manufacture. Since that time the evidence has become pretty strong that in 1952 the Soviets had not yet actually made, themselves, a single A-bomb. Their agents had simply walked off, from our atomic energy plants, with the parts needed, which had then been assembled in Russia into the bombs exploded for prestige purposes — or stockpiled for the future.

16. (Add mentally to Note 14 above.) Also, we know now that, if Taft had been nominated in 1952, the Soviets might have had reason to take the desperate gamble of military attack, before the weeding out of their agents and destruction of their power in this country could have begun under Taft as President. While by October, 1952, they had been relieved of this fear of Taft. And if they felt that they did not have nearly any such drastic opposition or dangerous setback to fear under Eisenhower, their appraisal of the situation has been amply justified by subsequent events. Any thought that the Communists are not immensely more powerful *within our country and within our government* today, than they were in 1952, is itself due to a blind complacency of the American people induced by that rising Communist influence.

But today, and for the immediately foreseeable future, I do not think any insults, threats, or opposition could provoke the Soviets into a full-scale hot war — despite all the advantages they would have from surprise attacks, and from methods and ruthlessness which civilized human beings could not use. For the present Communist rulers, unlike Stalin, are not only "mad, north-northwest." They fear the *simul-*

102

taneous uprising of so many hundreds of millions of enslaved people, at the automatic signal of an all-out war. And they are winning the rest of the planet too easily without it.

17. And this is just about what NATO has now cost us. The equivalent of our total *admitted* national debt. What do we have for it? Exactly what was originally planned – nothing.

18. As explained in the letter on the inside front cover, the reading list has been omitted in this edition because there are now so many better ones available.

19. If you are seriously interested in the more specific answers that can now be given you, as to what you as an individual can do about our danger – which has become so tremendously greater and more imminent since 1952 – write The John Birch Society, Belmont 78, Massachusetts. Doing so will entail no obligation on you of any kind.

CHIANG KAI-SHEK

A Personal Page

Dear Reader:

If the vagaries in our publishing pattern have not already sadly convinced you that we intend to run this magazine exactly as we please, this number will certainly do so.

Robert Browning was once asked the meaning of two lines of his poetry. He studied the verse for quite a while. "Madame," he replied finally, "when I wrote those lines only God and I knew what they meant. Now, I'm sorry to say, only God knows." Evidently my belief, on finishing any issue of ONE MAN'S OPINION, that at least the Good Lord and I both have some idea of what the next issue will be like, is unjustified presumption on my part.

For here is another pamphlet, when we firmly expected to return in this number to the regular format of the magazine. And, even more surprising, there is a reprint in this number of an article which appeared in an earlier one. But we set out to write the life of Chiang Kai-shek from 1927 to the present, as the feature article of a regular issue. We found that we needed the whole body of the magazine in order to tell even an intelligible story of what happened to Chiang, or of what Chiang caused to happen, during those thirty years. So we then decided to republish "The Early Years Of Chiang Kai-shek" in the same issue, to make our biographical sketch more complete, for present reading or for future reference.

This explanation still leaves three possible complaints which we should like to deflate by anticipation. (1) If you have already read the first and shorter article, and would find it tedious to do so again, we have a brilliant suggestion. Skip it, and begin this number on Page 9. (2) If you don't like paying for the same article twice, let us reassure you. It's a bonus! The main article, entirely new, covers thirty-two pages; and that is all our contract calls for anyway. (3) If your eyes are focused so intently on the Near East that you think these articles with a Far Eastern background are lacking in timeliness, we recommend that you merely read the magazine slowly. By the time you then finish the last page, things will probably be popping in the Far East again. The steam for such popping is certainly building up under the surface.

Sincerely,

Robert Welch

Foreword

On March 13 of this year the *Boston Traveler* carried a UP news item concerning one of Secretary Dulles' pronouncements about Red China. In this article appeared the statement: "The population of Formosa totals about eight million, most of whom would be happy if Chiang and his army went to China or anywhere else."

The ineffable absurdity of this statement is not important. The ease by which that absurdity could be proved – by asking a simple question, even by mail, of *any* ten men of the 7,500 Americans now in Formosa – is hardly more so. But the question as to why a writer for the United Press would make such a "smart-aleck crack" at Chiang is quite important indeed.

The basic reason is simple. Since 1924 the Kremlin's agents have been spreading lies about Chiang Kai-shek so industriously, in China and throughout the world, that their efforts have constituted a campaign of calumny unequalled in human experience. Directly and indirectly, with big lies and little lies spread by articulate thousands who had no knowledge of the ultimate source of their supposed facts and subtle innuendoes, that campaign has successfully darkened opinion about Chiang everywhere – until an undoubtedly honorable American reporter, who has probably never been within five thousand miles of Formosa, becomes an unwitting ally of the Communists in doing their dirty work for them.

There are two parallel results of this far-reaching attack on

Chiang, for our present purposes. One is that honest history concerning him has to be dug out from under the smearing layers of pro-Communist legend. The other is that, under these circumstances, the plain story of Chiang Kai-shek is bound to appear as eulogy. We want to assure our readers, therefore, that there is not, in a line we have written or failed to write, a single phrase consciously entered, omitted, distorted, or emphasized, so as to make the resulting impression fit any preconceived attitude about Chiang. We have presented as straightforward a record as our research could achieve.

Finally, we are sorry to be out of step with so many of the professional writers; or, as we see it, to have them out of step with us. There is little doubt that this biography will make John K. Fairbank, Owen Lattimore, Edgar Snow, Theodore White, Nym Wales, Vera Micheles Dean, Annalee Jacoby, Eleanor Lattimore, and other experts on China too numerous to list here, all choleric with anger. It will probably make their departed fellow expert, Agnes Smedley, turn over in her grave. But to bring about those unpleasant results has not been our objective. Our purpose was simply and solely to tell the truth about Chiang Kai-shek; as much of the truth as we could crowd into these pages, to as much of the American public as we could reach.

Part I: The Early Life Of Chiang Kai-shek

According to Chinese custom, whereby the day an individual is born is considered his first birthday, Chiang Kai-shek will be seventy years old at just about the time this magazine appears. He was born on October 31, 1887.

In 1954 Chiang was re-elected for a six-year term as the President of China. In principle his administration is still the legal government of all of China. Although, after 1945, the Communist rebels overran one province after another, pushing the Nationalist Government back until by 1950 it held only this one island province of Taiwan, Chiang and the Nationalists still think of the Chinese Communists as merely rebels against the Government, rather than as rulers of a now separate nation. They expect and intend, in due course, to subdue these rebels, and re-establish the legitimate Nationalist authority over all of their country. This principle of *de jure* government, however seemingly unrealistic in view of the present *de facto* control of the mainland by the Communists, is of extreme importance as a psychological weapon against the Communists in the present struggle for all of Asia.

The island of Taiwan, which we call Formosa, contains 13,886 square miles. Our contiguous states of Massachusetts, Connecticut, and Rhode Island together comprise an area of 13,864 square miles. In 1945, at the end of fifty years of Japanese rule of Taiwan, its population was about five million. Today, due to the addition of anti-Communist refugees from the mainland, the population is about eight million. This area and population make, quantitatively, a rather small holding to dignify by the name of "China," and from which to begin a restoration of control over the other thirty-four provinces. But on November 19, 1937, after Japan had captured Shanghai, was attacking Nanking, and beginning to pour troops into an occupation of China which took two million men, and lasted for eight years, Chiang made a statement for Tillman Durdin of the *New York Times*. At the end of that statement he said: "The enemy never realizes that China's territory is not conquerable. She is indestructible. As long as there is one spot in China free from enemy encroachment, the National Government will remain supreme." Today Chiang and his supporters consider that statement just as true with regard to the Communists as it was with regard to the Japanese nineteen years ago.

Because of this tenacity of his purpose; because of the loyalty to Chiang which is still such a powerful force throughout all of China; because of the sizable military strength still at his command; because of the showplace of democratic government, of freedom of individual movement and activity, and of self-sufficient prosperity by Asiatic standards, which he has made of Formosa, so near to the Communist mainland suffering near-starvation under murderous police-state rule; and because for thirty years Chiang has been the living symbol for all Asia of implacable opposition to the Communist terror; for all of these reasons, the Communists fear and hate Chiang Kai-shek today more than any other living man. They recognize in him their greatest enemy; the greatest danger to the maintenance of their present power, and the greatest obstacle to its further extension. Until Chiang is completely destroyed they can never rest easy, for he could at any time become the precipitating agent that began the turning of the whole tide against them.

Whether Chiang, and eventually we ourselves, succumb to

the Communists; or whether, by coming to our senses in time, and fighting for our lives by helping our friends to fight for us, we succeed in rolling back these barbarian forces and saving our civilization, Chiang Kai-shek will remain one of the great historical figures in any true record of the twentieth century. It is the purpose of this article to tell what little our skill and our space will permit about the earlier life of this proved leader of men, from his birth in 1887 to his marriage in December, 1927 — the same year, and the same month, when he finally stood forth as the acknowledged leader of his country.

II

In 1887 Grover Cleveland was serving his first term as president of the thirty-eight United States. In England the 3rd Marquis of Salisbury was prime minister, in between two of Gladstone's terms; and Queen Victoria celebrated her Golden Jubilee. William I yet reigned in Germany, while Bismarck ruled. Dom Pedro was still Emperor of Brazil, David Kalakaua was King of Hawaii, and the Emperor Kuang Hsu was in the twelfth year of his hen-pecked godship on the Manchu throne of China.

The Western world was not as ideologically tranquil as it seemed. The great twentieth-century struggle between free man and tyrant government, already foreshadowed by contemporary rumblings, was clearly foreseen by a few brilliant scholars such as Herbert Spencer. By 1887 Bismarck's academic stooges were already crystallizing some of the Marxian theories into legislation. In England the Fabian Society was already four years old. Even in America, in that very year, Edward Bellamy's *Looking Backward* was published; and Congress enacted the Interstate Commerce Act to regulate the railroads — that first long step in this country towards government interventionism. The truly perceptive could already hear the massive sandal of socialism set on stone, though far away.

But in China not only this fight between man and the state, over control of the industrial revolution and its benefits, was completely in the future; even the industrial revolution itself was as little known as the teachings of Karl Marx. In 1887 there was not a single mile of railroad in all of China, and even the trans-Siberian railroad was not to be started for four more years. The economy of the country was overwhelmingly agricultural. The state and means of communication were so poor that by 1887 many of the inhabitants of China were learning for the first time of the war their country had lost to France in 1885. All of the scientific and material advances of the West were to dawn on China almost simultaneously with the revolutionary ideas which elsewhere followed in their wake at a more comfortable distance. The sad result was that the gashes in the body and spirit of China, caused by the unending and bitter fight between the old and the new, have been deep, often recut, and at times all but fatal.

These circumstances go far to explain the motivations, the career, and the place in public esteem, of the man about whom we are writing. For it thus happened that the strength and influence of Chiang Kai-shek formed the irreplaceable suture, repeatedly holding together the wounded organism until it could at least partly heal, before some new blow broke open the old wounds or inflicted new ones. But for him his country, so weakened by internal strife and outside marauding without end, would have been swallowed up by Russia or Japan, or divided as spoils between them, long ago.

III

Chiang was born at Chikow, a small town in the coastal province of Chekiang. Due to his lifetime reticence concerning purely personal matters, the usual legends about a great man's childhood have had little soil on which to grow. His ancestors for generations had been farmers. His grandfather and father, while continuing as farmers, had won local reputations for some degree of scholarship. His family was comfortably prosperous until his father died, when Chiang was eight years old. After that his mother had to take on the burden of raising him, her two other children, and the son and daughter of Chiang's father by a former wife. The struggle against poverty, and against the attempted exploitation by neighbors of his mother's small property, left so lasting an impression on the youthful Chiang that he was to refer to them in a famous speech made fifty years later.

Nevertheless, his childhood was neither an abnormal nor an unhappy one. He had to help to sweep and cook and wash dishes, and he was brought up strictly, with no sparing of the rod for mischievous conduct. But he had plenty of opportunity to swim in the mountain streams which were a part of his immediate environment, to play the usual games of make-believe with other children, and to benefit from the teaching which his mother, a woman of some learning and exceptional character, added to the instruction he received in school.

The tremendous awakening of China to the ideas of the West was just beginning, and a spirit of rebellion against the despotism and stagnation of the decadent Manchu rule was stirring in the land. Both influences had reached young Chiang by the time he finished at the village schools in Chikow and was sent to high school in Fenghua. He became a serious student, somewhat aloof with his companions because of his lack of interest in their time-wasting occupations. He was already determined on a military career because of the revolutionary times which, even then, everybody could see were coming. And at the age of eighteen he publicly signalized his intention of studying abroad, to become a warrior of the revolution, by the almost sacrilegious and still dangerous act of cutting off his queue.

In May, 1906, the ambitious young man, with his mother making the necessary financial effort and sacrifices, went to

Japan to continue his education. Finding that he could not gain admittance to any military academy there except on the recommendation of his own government, Chiang returned to China, and prepared for the competitive examinations for entrance to Paoting Military Academy. After winning admission to Paoting he made such rapid and recognized progress that within a year he was one of the carefully chosen students certified to study military science in Japan. And so, by the summer of 1907, Chiang was back in Tokyo, in the preparatory military academy maintained there by the Chinese Ministry of War.

About sixty Chinese were being accorded this honor of studying military science in Japan at that time. But Chiang did not form close friendships with any of them, and this was only in part because of the "seriousness" which had kept him aloof in Fenghua. For now he had other immediate demands on his spare hours and energy. By the time he had moved on to regimental service in the Japanese Army, as a cadet-trainee for the Japanese Military College, Chiang was already in close association with Chen Chi-mei and other Chinese revolutionary leaders in Tokyo. He had met, and begun his discipleship to, Sun Yat-sen. But he did not neglect any of the opportunity provided him as a cadet. In later years the Japanese officers, under whom he served at this period, remembered him for conscientiousness rather than for brilliance, and for visible gratitude for all that he was taught. Not one of them had suspected that this young man, patiently accepting the rigorous discipline of an ordinary recruit in the Japanese 13th Field Artillery, was to become one of the oustanding generals and statesmen of his era.

IV

The "Double Ten," the tenth day of the tenth month, has become the Chinese national holiday because the first shot of the revolution that overthrew the Manchu dynasty was fired on October 10, 1911, at Wuchang. During the nineteenth century the Manchu emperors had suffered one humiliating defeat after another in their arms-length wars with European nations and Japan. They had submitted to degrading concessions of foreign privileges on Chinese soil, and had steadily lost power and prestige within China itself. Even the reactionary vigor of the incredible Dowager Empress T'ze Hsi had only delayed the deluge, which came three years after her death.

The father of the Chinese Revolution, Dr. Sun Yat-sen, had spent much time in Europe and America. As a consequence of his close association with socialist thinkers abroad, he early conceived of the revolution as economic as well as dynastic. And in 1905 he proclaimed the *Three People's Principles*, which have been the accepted core of Chinese social philosophy throughout all of the upheavals since. First of these principles was *Nationalism*; it called for a unified and independent China, ruled by a central government strong enough to withstand the imperialistic powers without and to control the provincial warlords within. Second was the principle of the *People's Sovereignty*; it called for a constitutional republican form of government, to be achieved after a period of tutelage under the revolutionary political party. Third was the principle of the *People's Livelihood*, whereby the government was to assume responsibility — in full accordance with socialist doctrine — for the economic well-being of its citizens; with especial emphasis on the redistribution of China's land to improve the condition of its vast farming population.

Chiang Kai-shek, as a devoted follower of Sun Yat-sen, has never wavered in his allegiance to these principles, nor in his drive towards the goals which they establish. From the very beginning he, as Dr. Sun before him, has never believed in the expropriation of land without proper payment to its former owners. (His remarkably fair and forward-looking solution of

115

China's "land problem," which he has put into effect in Formosa, is something we shall return to in a later article.) From the beginning he has believed that neither class warfare nor even class hatred was a necessary or desirable part of the Chinese Revolution. He has always believed that the *People's Sovereignty*, as he understood it, completely ruled out a police state — even for the sake of the guarantee of the *People's Livelihood*. But he still sincerely believes in the ultimate responsibility of the state for that livelihood, as set forth in this last of the *Three People's Principles*. To that extent he is, in philosophy and action, a socialist today. To that extent he and this writer would categorically disagree. For to us the people are responsible for the welfare and strength of their government, while the reverse should never be true.

But there was a circumstantial logic and historical inevitability in the appeal of socialism to a China in transition. The marvel is not that Chiang became doctrinally a socialist, but that: (1) he has combined so much common sense, dependence on individual initiative, and *true political liberalism*, with fundamental socialist dogma; and (2) that he has stood so firmly by the principle that socialism as a desirable end does not justify the use of barbaric means to achieve it or maintain it. And he was always much clearer on this latter all-important point than was his mentor, Dr. Sun.

On October 10, 1911, when the revolution broke, Chiang was in Tokyo. As soon as the news from Wuchang arrived, he and a companion asked for a forty-eight hour leave. They then borrowed enough money for civilian suits and for transportation, returned their uniforms and equipment by parcel post to their regimental headquarters, and took a boat for Shanghai. Although only twenty-four years old, Chiang was able to offer to the cause a degree of military training which was very rare among the revolutionaries. While Chen Chi-mei was seizing Shanghai itself, he assigned Chiang to lead a smaller force for the capture of Hangchow. That city being taken almost by sheer audacity, the young warrior was then made a regimental commander and put in charge of training troops for the next stage of the revolution. The next stage, and the next, for a dozen years, were mostly rearrangements of confusion. The scholarly but inefficient Sun Yat-sen gradually lost control of the revolution to Yuan Shih-kai. His Kuomintang (National People's Party) was outlawed and driven underground. The power of the everfighting provincial warlords steadily rose through all of the changes in the picture. An entirely separate government was set up in North China. But the recovering Kuomintang slowly established some semblance of a republic in the South, with Canton as the capital and Dr. Sun as president. During all of these years and events Chiang Kai-shek's dedication and ability became ever more widely recognized, until he was one of four men who shared the top authority and responsibility under Dr. Sun himself. And in 1923, when Moscow was making strenuous efforts to pull Dr. Sun and his Canton government into the Soviet orbit, Chiang was sent to Russia. Armed with letters to Lenin, Trotsky, and Chicherin, he was to study the Soviet system, and to appraise the advantages for China of a "friendly working arrangement" with the Communist leaders.

Chiang saw the "old Bolsheviks" at a time when some idealistic fervor still shone through the hardening bureaucratic tyranny. Himself a still young and enthusiastic revolutionary, he was impressed. But he also saw many of the faults, and much of the unsuitability for China, of the Communist program. After four months in Russia he brought back a report containing these unfavorable reactions, while still advocating adoption by the Kuomingtang of many organizational procedures he had observed in Moscow. And he did not yet actively oppose the "help" and influence of Borodin, Bluecher, Earl Browder, and other Communist

117

advisers, who were infiltrating the top levels of the Kuomintang with the intention of taking over the whole Chinese Revolution.

V

Dr. Sun Yat-sen died on March 12, 1925, in Peking, while engaged in futile efforts to bring about a unification of the northern and southern governments. His death, without any successor designated among the four leading aspirants, left his "republic" in the South subject to severe factional disturbances; subject to great danger from the ambitious warlords in these southern provinces; and subject to increased efforts on the part of the now powerful Communists to seize the opportunity offered them by so chaotic a situation. Armies marched and fought, under generals who shifted their allegiance from one leader or alliance of leaders to another, in a confusion almost beyond belief.

Chiang Kai-shek had several advantages over all of the other actors on the scene, however, which enabled him to save the Kuomintang from disintegration and to emerge as Dr. Sun's undisputed heir. Besides his superior general ability, he had a specific ability to work with each or all of his rivals, for the common cause, which none of the others possessed. He showed both great skill and equal determination in avoiding an open break with the Communists, and in using their collaboration, without ever letting them get the upper hand. Perhaps most important of all, at this particular juncture, he had under his command the one unwaveringly loyal and really effective – although still small – military force in the field. His First Army Corps was built around the young officers who were graduates of the Whampoa Military Academy, of which Chiang had been president since its founding by Sun Yat-sen in June, 1924.

For many months Chiang had given all of his time and energy to getting this school started on the right track.

118

Taking tremendous interest in the military training, the political indoctrination, and the personal lives of his cadets, he had been pushing groups of four hundred through the intensive training course every ten or twelve weeks. The "Whampoa Cadets," always loyal to Chiang, were henceforth to play an extremely important part in the military history of China. Already, by the summer of 1925, they were the inner strength of the 7,000-man force which enabled Chiang to clean up the situation in Kwangtung Province, of which Canton was the capital, and to proceed on this secure military base to the consolidation of the Kuomintang's control over the other southern provinces.

By the summer of 1926 Chiang felt ready for the "Northern Expedition" which he had long planned. This was the seemingly impossible undertaking to compel, by military conquest, the rival government at Peking and the warlords of the northern provinces to accept the Canton organization as the central and legitimate government for all of China. The numerical strength of the Peking forces was so superior to anything Chiang could lead on so long a march against them, that the northern government and its allied warlords were contemptuous of the danger. Also, by now Borodin and his confederates had won over so many converts within the Kuomintang itself, and made themselves so powerful, that the division within the party doubled the problems Chiang would have to face in his Northern Expedition — especially since Borodin bitterly opposed it. The last thing the Russians wanted, at this point, was a successful expedition of this kind, and the unification of a disordered and divided China under the hegemony of Chiang Kai-shek. Which was undoubtedly one of the reasons why Chiang considered it imperative to make the effort when he did.

The showdown with the Communists came right in the midst of the campaign. Borodin, recognizing Chiang as the strong man of the future, had long hoped to win him over to the Russian side. Finally realizing that he would never succeed, he took advantage of Chiang's absence in the North, and preoccupation with the problems there, to bring off a coup d'état. He seized the reins of power and established a Communist-controlled government in southern China. This was the nearest Moscow was to come to making the mainland of China a Soviet satellite, for a quarter of a century.

While Chiang undoubtedly would have preferred that the break come later, he didn't hesitate to accept the challenge. And, to condense volumes of history into a paragraph, he was brilliantly successful in overcoming both his internal and external enemies. Interrupting the Northern Expedition long enough, he overthrew and mopped up the Communists, expelled Borodin and his foreign associates from the country, expelled Mao Tze-tung and his Chinese Communist associates from the Kuomintang, and re-established the southern government firmly under the control of his own allies and supporters. Then he returned to the North. With the combination of military skill and of the political appeal of the *Three People's Principles* — which his civilian appointees carried to the inhabitants of the northern provinces simultaneously with the arrival of his troops — he won through to at least a tenuous unification of China under a theoretically republican form of government. His next great ambition was to consolidate that unification, carry the country through the necessary political tutelage envisioned by Sun Yat-sen, and establish a truly republican China in its proper place among the democratic nations of the world.

VI

Among the tremendous events compressed into so few sentences above was the temporary withdrawal of Chiang Kai-shek, in 1927, from both military command and participation in the government. This he had done as a means of bringing about harmony between his faction of the Kuomintang, which had moved its seat of power from Canton to the ancient Chinese capital of Nanking, and the opposing faction which, while dominated by the Communists, had set up a rival government under Wang Ching-wei, at Hankow. Even after the disillusioned Wang had helped to drive out the Communists, the two capitals remained, with rival armies in the field; both armies supposedly fighting the northern warlords but in far more danger of fighting each other. Chiang stepped down, in order to make a reunification easier, and retired to his native hills in Chekiang. This interlude has to be snatched back from the general sweep of our historical broom, because within it occurred an all-important episode in Chiang's personal life that requires our close attention.

In accordance with Chinese custom Chiang's mother had selected a wife for him when he was fifteen years old. The couple had had one son, Chiang Ching-kuo – who is a very able lieutenant of his father on Taiwan today. But the marriage had taken place even before Chiang went to school in Japan. His wife, with no interest in political affairs, had wanted Chiang to give up his military career and remain at home. This was not unreasonable from her point of view, but impossible from his. And the impasse had led to an amicably arranged divorce in the early 1920's.

Not long thereafter, at the home of Dr. Sun in Canton, Chiang met Mayling Soong, youngest daughter of a fabulous family. Her father, Charles Soong, had been one of the first Chinese to acquire a college education in America. He had become an ordained Christian minister. Then he had returned to China, to propagate the gospel, to become a wealthy manufacturer, to raise six children, and to develop into one of his country's leading citizens. His oldest son, T.V. Soong, was Minister of Finance in the Nationalist Government in 1927, later became Prime Minister, and is today internationally known as a financier. The two other sons, T.L. Soong and T.A. Soong, both also later became prominent in banking

121

and industry. But the three daughters achieved even more fame for the family. Eling, oldest of the sisters, had married H.H. Kung, long active in the Chinese Government as well as in international banking, and now retired. The middle sister, Chingling, was the wife of Dr. Sun Yat-sen. She sided with the Communists, when the break came in the Kuomintang after her husband's death, and since 1940 has been an ardent supporter of the Soviet, with her home in Moscow. The youngest sister, Mayling, had come to America for her education, graduated from Wellesley College, and returned to China thoroughly westernized. In 1927 she was living with her widowed mother, who was as devout a Christian as had been the Rev. Soong himself, in their home near Kobe, in Japan.

Chiang had fallen in love, in the Western style of romantic deference hardly to have been expected in view of his background, with Mayling Soong. There had been a great exchange of correspondence for years, leaving no doubt that she reciprocated the feeling. The question was whether her mother would consent to the marriage. One month after Chiang began his retirement in Chekiang, he left for Japan to find out. Mrs. Soong was known to have opposed the match because of Chiang's first wife, because he was at least a dozen years older than her daughter, and because she had a dislike for the soldierly caste. But the real obstacle was the difference in religion. When Chiang finally obtained his interview with Mrs. Soong she asked him point blank if he was willing to become a Christian. He simply said that he didn't know, and could make no promise; that he would study Christianity earnestly, but accept it only if he became a sincere convert. This honest answer completely won over Mrs. Soong, and the engagement was announced.

The wedding took place in Shanghai on December 1, 1927. It consisted of a private Christian religious service, in the Soong home on Seymour Road; and a public service, Chinese style, in the ballroom of the Majestic Hotel. There were thirteen hundred guests present, and the event was important news in the foreign press as well as in the papers of China. Chiang issued a public statement, pledging the devotion of his bride and himself to the cause of the Chinese Revolution, and the couple went to the hills and lakes of Chekiang for their honeymoon.

It was not until the fall of 1928, after a thorough study of the Bible and much soul-searching, that Chiang was baptized into the Christian Church. He had refused to be hurried, even by his wife. But when he did become a Christian it was with a wholehearted consecration that has never wavered. To him his faith has remained an inspiration, a solace, and a guide, throughout every day of his life.

As to his marriage, few famous unions have worked out so happily, or withstood terrific stress with such complete success. During nearly thirty years Madame Chiang has labored and planned with her husband, through storms within her family and the shifting loyalties of friends, through political intrigues and diplomatic crises, through civil wars and foreign wars that engulfed their country, through moments of triumph and years of disaster. The smears and lies about their personal relations, planted cleverly and spread vigorously by the Communists, have left the ardent affection of their private lives, and the solidarity of their public efforts, still unharmed.

These slanders have, of course, been but one small part of the longest, most vicious, most widespread, and most determined smear campaign in all history. During three or four years around 1940 Stalin desperately needed to have the Japanese armies remain bogged down in China, and it was the never-give-up policy of Chiang Kai-shek which held them there. So for that brief period the Communist hounds were called off, both from their wolf-pack attacks on Chiang in China, and their worldwide yapping about him. With the exception of this one lull, however, the size and character of the campaign have been such as to give all of the Western world, and especially America, a continuously and infamously distorted view of a great Christian statesman. That campaign was already under way by the time of his marriage. For the part Chiang was destined to play, as the ideological, political, and military enemy of the Communists during the decades to come, could already be foreseen. His honeymoon had lasted only ten days when a Preliminary Meeting of the Plenary Session of the Kuomintang's Central Executive Committee, called because of the way both the military and political situation were deteriorating, unanimously voted to restore him as Commander-in-Chief of the National Revolutionary Army. Seven days later, on December 17, 1927, Chiang was made the actual head of the political side of the government as well. His preponderant authority in the Kuomintang, and in China itself, was now unmistakably established; and the period of his true greatness had begun.

Part II: The Years Of Greatness

Since my visit to Taiwan (Formosa) was made specifically for its background value in preparing this article, the reader is humbly requested to forgive the necessary intrusion of personal experience and the personal pronoun in just two or three paragraphs telling about that visit. The kindness and hospitality with which your editor was received, and the opportunities given him to see and do so much in so comparatively short a time, need to be mentioned, even at the regrettable expense of making him sound a lot more important than he was, or is.

For while only a few of the high officials of the Chinese Government were aware that one of my small books, strongly supporting Chiang Kai-shek, had been translated into Chinese and was in official use by their own Education Department, they all knew that — for whatever it was worth — I was an earnest anti-Communist and a friend of Free China. So they went out of their way, not only to see that I was looked after and entertained properly, but to spare me adequate time for private interviews. My conversations with Vice-President Chen Cheng and Defense Minister Yu Ta-wei, in particular, were long, more confidential than might reasonably have been expected, extremely interesting, and much appreciated. Madame Chiang graciously invited me to have tea with her, and an hour of private discussion, at her home on top of Yangmingshan.

But of course the highlight of the trip was my interview

with President Chiang Kai-shek. It took place in his office at government headquarters in Taipei, and there were several aides and dignitaries present. The conversation, nevertheless, was strictly between the two of us. The Honorable Sampson Shen, the most marvelous linguist with whom I had ever come in contact — and now Director of the Government Information Office — acted as interpreter.

The Generalissimo was most cordial, and the conversation could probably have taken almost any turn I wished. And a professional journalist, or even a good amateur, would undoubtedly have had a lot of penetrating questions all prepared. But it seemed to me unlikely that the Generalissimo could or would dare tell me, a private citizen, under the circumstances and in the time he could give me, anything which I could not readily learn from other sources. So I had deliberately decided to sacrifice the opportunity of asking questions, for the sake of giving him a message; one which, coming from an American private citizen, who could speak only on behalf of himself and other private citizens, might still convey a tiny measure of welcome encouragement. And the gist of my near-monologue — punctuated every two or three minutes by translations of its parts, and by occasional questions from my patient listener — might be ruthlessly condensed into approximately the following:

"Many Americans share your belief that there is yet time for the Chinese Nationalist Government to return to the mainland, drive the Communists out, and re-establish a truly republican government over your whole country. I am one of a great many Americans who not only believe this, but who are determined to help, in every way such individuals can help, to create the climate and the opportunity that will make this possible. This is not, however, primarily because of our sympathy for China or the Chinese people, as much as our humanitarian instincts also support that attitude. Our chief worry is with regard to our own country. Our interest in helping Nationalist China is in thereby helping ourselves. We are convinced that our interests and your interests now happen completely to coincide; that the stronger you and your government become, the more defense Nationalist China offers as a bulwark between the Communists and ourselves. This purely selfish feeling on our part is far more important than our altruistic concern with the plight of your own suffering countrymen. And for this very reason, because our efforts are motivated by self-interest, you can count more surely on their vigor, their consistency, and their sincerity. We like China and the Chinese. But with us, and in our thinking, America comes first, just as we are sure China does and should come first in your own."

Now what this lone American businessman said to the President of China wouldn't be worth repeating, or giving three lines even in this magazine, but for one thing. That — which is the essence of, and a chief reason for, this prelude — was the Generalissimo's reaction to the above confession. There was no slightest doubt that he was extremely pleased to hear this point of view so plainly expressed. And the experience emphasizes an obvious truth that our government persistently disregards. Nobody, except power-seeking hypocrites within foreign governments who wish to strengthen their personal positions by the use of our money, gives a hurrah about our being such great, benevolent, and unselfish Samaritans. For the little people we really and unselfishly would like to help seldom hear about it and wouldn't believe it anyway. Not altruism, but an *enlightened* and firm *self-interest* on the part of the United States is all our true anti-Communist friends and allies really want, anywhere in the world. And that is the one thing we haven't offered, or shown any trace of having, in at least twelve long years.

Nor is this point at all irrelevant in the introductory paragraphs to "the later years of Chiang Kai-shek." For during the three decades covered by this article the threads of his fate have been increasingly, and at last inextricably, interwoven with the threads of American foreign policy. And if American foreign policy throughout the last half of that period had been based honestly and frankly on self-interest, instead of on star-gazing theories of "democratizing" and uplift g the whole world by meddling in everybody else's business, many suffering nations would be in a far happier position than they are now. This is most true of China. If such careful common sense had prevailed, there can hardly be any doubt that Chiang Kai-shek would today be solidly established in Nanking or Peiping as the president of a united and prosperous republic of five hundred million Chinese; or that these hard-working family-loving people, gradually absorbing into the best of their own traditional customs the new industrial ways and modern thinking of the West, would be firm friends and great admirers of our country. For much of the story of Chiang Kai-shek is the tragedy of what might have been, for China and for himself, but for the follies and crimes of our government.

II
THE WARLORDS COMBINE

In the earlier years of this period, however, there were other forces at work, with regard to which American influence was remote, indirect, and relatively unimportant. After Chiang had taken the revolution started by Sun Yat-sen out of the hands of the usurping Communists, in 1927, and in his ensuing effort to make of China a unified constitutionally governed nation, the first of the major obstacles he had to overcome was the ever-recurring, always the same but always different, resistance of the warlords. During the long and incredibly confused civil war which had followed the fall of the Manchu dynasty in 1911, the power and personal jealousies and claims to varying degrees of independence, on the part of these "tuchuns", had become the most important consideration in any study of the Chinese political landscape. For China, which is twenty-five percent larger in area than the mainland United States, is broken by high mountain ranges and huge rivers into many geographical divisions. And at that time it was almost entirely agricultural, had almost no passable highways outside of its large cities, possessed only five thousand miles of railroad in the whole country, and had an extremely primitive communications system. It was almost inevitable, therefore, that various areas would fall under the sway of local feudal rulers; and that the ever-shifting loyalties and alliances of these indigenous warlords should make the establishment of a firm central government difficult to achieve and even more difficult to maintain. When, on July 5, 1928, Chiang Kai-shek brought the famous Northern Expedition to an end with the capture of Peking (which was then renamed Peiping, meaning "Northern Peace"), he completed a military campaign for unification which had started from Canton, fifteen hundred miles to the south, two years before. He thus accomplished the first even theoretical union of north China and south China in the seventeen years since the revolution had begun. But the insubordination and wavering allegiances of the warlords who were within the fold, the hostility of those still outside, the tenuous weakness of any national governmental organization, and the factionalism within his own Kuomintang (National People's Party) made even this claim to unification an ephemeral phantom that was likely to disappear at any minute. Chiang now had before him the extremely arduous job of establishing the authority of the Nanking government as in fact the government of all of China.

In the southern provinces there was a group of powerful and almost autonomous warlords, led by Li Tsung-jen, who had supported Chiang throughout the Northern Expedition, but who had no intention of paying taxes or otherwise subordinating themselves and their armies to a national government. A wide swath of central north China, from Shantung Province on the Yellow Sea, all the way across to Chinghai and Ninghsia Provinces, more than a thousand miles to the west, was under the military control of Feng Yu-hsiang, the notorious and slippery "Christian General," with his mercenary army of four hundred thousand men. Roughly north of this elongated empire, in parts or all of the provinces of Shansi, Hopei, Chahar, and Suiyuan, General Yen Hsi-shan exercised both military and economic dictatorship. Northernmost of all was Manchuria, already more industrialized than any other part of China, under the rule of Chang Hsueh-liang, the famous "Young Marshal." He had inherited the provinces from his even more famous father, Chang Tso-lin, and had a more "legitimate" claim to his position and to the autonomy of his government than any of the other warlords. Within the Kuomintang itself there were enmities and rivalries, which had intermittently been glossed over for the sake of carrying out the Northern Expedition, between rightwing groups containing at least one leader who still expected to emerge as the ruler of all China, if and when unification became a reality. Much of the whole left-wing faction, in particular, was always willing to listen to the schemes of Wang Ching-wei, even though he usually concocted those schemes while in Europe; and to rally behind him every time he came back to China with the ambitious intention of taking Chiang Kai-shek's place.

For more than two years after the fall of Peking, the permutations and combinations of these warlords and political chieftains, in their efforts either to replace Chiang or simply to establish permanent principalities or niches for themselves, were too kaleidoscopic to be outlined here. With just two exceptions, nothing and nobody among the major materials for this kaleidoscope ever stayed put for more than a few months at the time. The first exception was Chiang himself. He never lost sight of the goal, which he had inherited from Sun Yat-sen, of a unified republic of China. And although he made it clear time after time that he was entirely willing for somebody other than himself to be the head of such a republic, he was never willing to accept any compromise or any arrangement short of that ultimate goal, no matter how overwhelming appeared the current assemblage of forces against him. The second exception was Chang Hsueh-liang, the new ruler of Manchuria. The "Young Marshal," after early negotiations with Chiang, agreed to unite his domain with the rest of China under the republican regime, and the Kuomintang flag was raised over his capital city of Mukden on December 29, 1928. He then remained a loyal supporter of Generalissimo Chiang Kai-shek throughout all this period of strife — and until the tragic Sian incident of several years later.

And Recombine . . .

With all of the others Chiang used diplomacy when he could, and force when he had to fight. He put down separate rebellions and joint rebellions and new governments and seizures of power within his own government, almost monthly. Until eventually, early in 1930, nearly all of his enemies, on all sides, rose simultaneously in a concerted effort to crush him. Even Wang Ching-wei rushed from Europe to Hongkong, and thence to Peiping, where he got together an "Enlarged Plenary Session" of the Kuomintang which declared itself the new "National Government." In it were such important figures as Yen Hsi-shan, Feng Yu-hsiang, and Li Tsung-jen. This combination, in which the most powerful warlords of both South and North took part, with the second most important political figure in the Kuomintang itself — Wang Ching-wei — as their leader, brought on a few months of the bloodiest war China had seen in the eighty years since the Taiping Rebellion.

But again the "Young Marshal" refused to join the

coalition. Many of the peoples in the provinces of these warlords, and even many of the soldiers and officers in their armies, had by this time come to have great respect for the kind of government Chiang was trying to institute whenever he had the opportunity. And the military and diplomatic skill of the one strong leader, Chiang, was far superior to that arrived at by the jealous cooperation of his opponents. So at last, by the end of 1930, this final great civil war, on the Kuomintang road to the re-establishment of China as one nation, was over — though at a cost during the last six months of approximately two hundred thousand lives. Even all of this terrible strife and destruction did not mean that warlordism now disappeared from the Chinese scene; nor that, on the slightest word from Chiang Kai-shek, the remaining warlords now disbanded their local troops or paid over to the central government the taxes they collected. But it did mean that from 1931 on there was again such a nation as China, with one recognized government which could speak for that nation. It meant that insubordination of the warlords and insurrections (except of the Communists) now receded in importance among the problems that Chiang faced. But several other great problems, unfortunately, were already and simultaneously pushing at the door.

III
THE STRUGGLE WITH JAPAN

One of the most serious of these problems was Japanese imperialist ambition. Japan had taken possession of the island of Taiwan (Formosa) and made it a Japanese territory in 1895. It had established its first real foothold on the Asiatic mainland by seizing physical control of the reigning family of the ancient kingdom of Korea, and military control of the area, in 1905; and by officially making the whole Korean peninsula a province of Japan in 1910. But Formosa and Korea were very small stopgaps, towards making room for the expanding population, industrial needs, and political ego of Japan. And the sheer geography of the situation showed that the only place for Tokyo to turn, for further conquests, was to the territories of China. This not only caused Japan to be an enemy of any China that might exist as a nation, and to be opposed to the unification of that nation. It also meant that Japan was an early and active enemy of Chiang Kai-shek, as the one strong man who might in time make China itself strong enough to resist Japanese encroachment.

As early as 1928 Japan had tried to make trouble for Chiang, during the Northern Expedition. With Japanese forces on the Shantung peninsula it had blocked the march of his army to Peking. Chiang had kept his head, however, and refused to get embroiled. He captured Peking anyway, and handled the whole matter so skillfully that on March 28, 1929 Japan agreed to withdraw all of its troops from Shantung.

But Japan's aggressive intentions and actions in Manchuria were far more serious. For years, with the complacent consent of the "Old Marshal," Chang Tso-lin, Japan had infiltrated and industrialized that huge northern territory; and had offered no objection to the purely theoretical sovereignty, over Chang and his provinces, of whatever government there happened to be in Nanking or Canton or Peking or anywhere else. But the "Young Marshal," Chang Hsueh-liang, reversed his father's policy. Despite Japanese pressures, he allied himself with and supported Chiang Kai-shek in the final great flare-up of the civil wars which we have just described. And so, in 1931, when Chang Hsueh-liang left his .provinces unguarded, in order to hold the republican line in north China while the Generalissimo finished up his troubles with the warlords in the South, Japan moved in. With a lightning stroke of the "Kwantung Army," which had been maintained in the leased Port Arthur area, the Japanese seized the capital city of Mukden, barred Chang

Hsueh-liang's return to Manchuria, and began to spread their occupation forces throughout the whole territory.

The League Labors And Brings Forth A Mouse . . .

Chiang Kai-shek simply was not strong enough at that time, militarily or politically, to undertake war with Japan or the recapture of Manchuria. So he referred the whole matter to the League of Nations, as the only course holding out any hope at all under the circumstances. The League went through the motions to be expected, and appointed the Lytton Commission to investigate. The Commission went through its own motions, and twelve months later issued its report that Japan should not keep Manchuria! In the meantime the Japanese had set up local governments of Chinese collaborators all over the provinces; had captured the last remaining strongholds held by forces loyal to the "Young Marshal"; had combined its puppet governments into the "independent republic" of Manchukuo; had made Henry Pu Yi, the deposed last Manchu emperor of China, regent of the new "republic"; and, on September 15, 1932, had extended official recognition to Manchukuo as a new nation. As Hollington Tong says, "the net result of all the League's intervention was to leave Manchuria just where the Lytton Commission found it – in the grip of the Japanese." (And in 1934 Japan was to tighten this grip by converting the puppet state into an empire, with Henry Pu Yi as "emperor."

In the meantime, on December 15, 1931, Chiang had resigned all of his offices in the National Government and temporarily retired. This was a course he had taken before, and would take on other occasions in the future, whenever it seemed to him that his withdrawal would eliminate bitterness, promote unity in the Kuomintang, and benefit China in the long run. Taking advantage of Chiang's absence, however, the Japanese Navy, on January 28, 1932, had attacked Shanghai itself. It had accompanied the attack with a bombing, at four-thirty in the morning, of the main Chinese section of the city. This barbarous action took thousands of lives, and drove 250,000 fugitives to the shelter of the International Settlements. In due course Japan actually captured Shanghai. But the pressure of the international representatives forced her to pull her troops out again, and the evacuation was completed in May. The face-losing results of this rash adventure by the Japanese Navy undoubtedly constituted one reason why the Army clique, now in control in Tokyo, pushed the consolidation of its position in Manchuria so hard, as outlined above – and then went on from Manchuria, during 1933, to seize the adjoining province of Jehol.

Chiang was now back as head of the Nanking government. But he was without hope of any help from the foreign powers to prevent Japan advancing further into Chinese territory. The Communists were making serious trouble in Kiangsi and adjoining provinces. China's military and economic forces were entirely inadequate for an all-out war with Japan, and there was urgent need for time in which to continue the unifying and strengthening process before this inevitable war did come. Under these circumstances Chiang took the very unpopular course of suing for a truce. Japan enforced very hard terms. Then, when Chiang was confronted with a rebellion in Fukien Province, she ignored the truce she had already signed, and made those terms even more harsh. The chief effect of the settlement was to leave Japan in position to go to work in the provinces of Hopei (which contained Peiping), Chahar, Suiyuan, Shansi, and Shantung, with opportunistic Chinese collaborators, to set up another Japanese puppet state similar to Manchukuo further north.

The Warlords Again . . .

The patriotic bitterness against Japan soon became so widespread, throughout China, that it actually played right

135

into the Japanese hands. For all of the disgruntled warlords who had been defeated in the 1929-31 struggles now seized upon the unpopularity of Chiang's position as offering the chance to oust him. From Feng Yu-hsiang in the North to Li Tsung-jen in the South, they began organizing "Anti-Japanese National Salvation Forces," and similarly named armies, ostensibly to fight Japan. But their first and main objective was to supplant Chiang Kai-shek. How untrustworthy the announced intentions were is made clear by the fact that most of the guns and ammunition with which these armies were equipped, supposedly to fight the Japanese, were sold to them, gladly and promptly, by Japan! The imperialists in Tokyo were not fooling. They were earnestly determined to get rid of Chiang Kai-shek, to disrupt China completely, and to swallow it all up, province by province.

Fortunately, large numbers of the soldiers and officers pulled into these "anti-Japanese armies" refused to support the scheme, or actually went over to Chiang when they saw how the land lay. Also, as usual, the various warlords very soon took to squabbling among themselves. And a plenary session of the Kuomintang Central Executive Committee strongly supported Chiang's policies. So the whole movement fell apart. Equally fortunately, Chiang handled the insurgent generals with great wisdom and generosity. For some of them, and Li Tsung-jen in particular, proved to be towers of strength for the national government when the all-out war with Japan did ultimately come.

That such a war could not be far off was now evident to everybody. One reason was that, despite all of these internal disorders, despite the even more serious and persistent drain by the Communists on the government's resources and energies (which will be discussed later), and despite the terrific handicaps imposed by the Japanese occupation of important provinces, China was making remarkable economic and spiritual progress as a nation; so much and such rapid progress under Chiang Kai-shek's inspired and energetic leadership that the Japanese did not dare wait much longer. All during 1936, while special envoys of Japan and China worked with painful futility at the impasse created by Japanese ambition and Chinese patriotism, the outlook grew steadily darker. Then, in December of that year, occurred the famous and incredible Sian Incident. Chiang was kidnapped and held prisoner for two weeks by two of his own generals, Chang Hsueh-liang and Yang Hu-cheng. The results were surprising and revealing, at least to Japan. There was a spontaneous upsurge of tremendous support for Chiang and of condemnation of the misguided insurgents by the whole population. The Nanking government proved its ability to function smoothly and to keep the country utterly pacified while its leader was known to be in hourly danger of death. And at last the rebellious generals surrendered of their own accord *to their captive.* All of this showed how immeasurably the unification of the country, in spirit and in loyalty to Chiang Kai-shek, had proceeded since the abortive efforts against him of not much more than a year before. The Sian affair helped to hasten the Japanese decision, and Tokyo's military leaders began to look for a convenient incident with which to precipitate hostilities.

Japan Starts The War . . .

That incident came on the night of July 7, 1937, in a clash between a detachment of Japanese occupation troops and a detachment of China's 29th Army, near the Marco Polo Bridge fifteen miles from Peiping. Japan quickly mobilized forces in the Peiping area, and on August 13 began its attack on Shanghai. Three months were required to take the city. Then the Japanese armies immediately pushed on towards Nanking, and the full-scale invasion of China was under way. By the time we were attacked at Pearl Harbor, on December 7, 1941, China had already been at war with Japan for four and one-half years; and had actually been fighting against Japanese seizures of Chinese territory for the ten years since 1931.

By 1941 Japan occupied all of north China and most of the coastal provinces in the South. It had set up and recognized its puppet government of China, in Nanking, under Wang Ching-wei. It was regularly and mercilessly bombing Chungking, the temporary capital to which Chiang had retreated, a thousand miles inland from Nanking. Nevertheless, during that year the Tokyo government made increasingly desperate overtures to find peace terms which Chiang Kai-shek would accept. Japan wanted to end the "China incident" before embroiling itself in the war with England and the United States which it knew was coming. Chiang was positive that these efforts and the ultimate intentions of the Japanese were not to be trusted. He also could read the signs, and had made up his mind to cast China's lot with those of America and England. On December 8, 1941, one day after the bombing of Pearl Harbor, his government officially declared war on Germany and Italy, and Chiang sent to President Roosevelt the following brief but emotion-packed telegram:

> To our new common battle we offer all we are and all we have, to stand with you until the Pacific and the world are freed from the curse of brute force and endless perfidy.

By this courageous action Chiang committed himself and his people to four more years of a terrible ordeal for China. For, although it had been Japan, not Germany, which had attacked us, the Communist influences within our government were so strong that we made a step-child of the war with Japan. We not only devoted almost all of our resources and energies to the war in Europe, but especially to defending Russia from the Germans. At this same time, however, in Chiang's part of the world, our ally Russia, whom we were thus defending in Europe, reconfirmed its friendly neutrality pact with our enemy Japan, to give Japan a free hand to destroy our ally, China.

But this was only one small part of the unfair burden Chiang had to bear. Although he was officially appointed Supreme Commander for the Allied Powers in the China Theatre (which included contiguous areas outside of China), the man sent to serve as his Chief-of-Staff and to command the American forces under him was Lt. General Joseph W. Stilwell. The most charitable thing that can be said about the opinionated, egotistical, and incompetent Stilwell is that he was a boy sent to do a man's job. What's more, while the lend-lease materials supplied to all of our other allies were turned over to their governments for dispositoin, those for China were put in Stilwell's hands to be dribbled out to Chiang Kai-shek as he saw fit. And since, as revealed by Stilwell's own diary, his greatest pleasure in life was in finding ways to humiliate Chiang Kai-shek, his military superior whom he was supposed to be trying to help, this control of materials so desperately needed was a powerful weapon in his malicious hands.

Not that the American troops to be commanded in the China theatre, or the materials supplied to Chiang, amounted to very much. For again, due to Communist influences, while the United States was pouring millions of men and billions of dollars' worth of goods into the fight in Europe, she was starving even MacArthur's command in the South Pacific for both; and she was treating Chiang's theatre even worse. Up to the end of 1944, less than five percent of America's total lend-lease supplies of war materiel to its allies had been consigned to China; and most of these supplies were usually snatched away somewhere en route to China for other "emergency" needs. The underlying explanation of these developments is that Russia wanted to keep the war between

China and Japan – and between America and Japan – going just as long as it possibly could, for its own purposes, and that the Communists had enough influence in Washington to guide events in that direction.

Japan Loses The War . . .

This is all the more shameful when the stark fact is considered that, throughout these nearly four years we were in World War II, Chiang was by far our most effective ally; and that he remained our staunch ally despite many opportunities to make a separate peace with Japan on favorable terms. But for the immeasurable drain on Japanese strength which Chiang's unceasing resistance required, there is no telling what might have happened to Australia or Hawaii, or even to our West Coast, during those same years when the Japanese did take over Hongkong, Indonesia, and the Philippines. The size of the part Chiang Kai-shek played in this total picture can best be indicated by the number of Japanese military and occupational personnel which he kept bogged down in China. When the war was over, despite all the tens of thousands of Japanese that had been killed in the actual fighting, and despite whatever forces had been pulled out for more urgent needs elsewhere during the last months of the war, the number of the Japanese soldiers, administrators, technicians, and other officials that were actually evacuated from China – according to the official figures of our government, which handled the evacuation – was 2,986,438. And approximately one half of these men were uniformed troops.

Eventually, however, despite everything Russia could do to keep the war in Asia going, even months after Japan was trying so hard to surrender, the end of the long struggle did come. Japan was beaten, her soldiers and commissars were shipped home, and this great obstacle to a united republican China was removed. It seemed that peace with Japan might at last make it possible for Chiang to establish his country, resilient from its wounds and proudly cohesive after its victorious sacrifices, in its rightful place among the great nations. But there was still another enemy which had been working against this result for twenty years; an enemy which now began — with the increasing connivance of our government from 1943 on — to loom as an ever more dangerous threat to Chiang's hopes and plans for his country. To present that part of the history of Chiang Kai-shek, and of China, we have to go back to 1927, and retrace our journey along another path.

IV
THE COMMUNISTS AGAIN

Lenin himself had plotted and expected that, after Russia, China would be the next great nation to be taken over by the Communists. Hardly had the first dust of the Russian Revolution settled in Leningrad and Moscow before Communist agents went to work on China, which was already in the long throes of its own chaotic revolution. The early progress of this work was quite encouraging to the Kremlin. For the socialistic beliefs of Dr. Sun Yat-sen made him too ready to cooperate with, and accept help from, the Communists. The whole Chinese situation was extremely confused, and the Communists fish best in the muddiest waters. And the Soviet agents sent to China at this time, such as Borodin, General Bluecher, and Earl Browder, were skillful revolutionaries. Due to these and other causes, the whole force of the Chinese Revolution might have been consolidated behind Communist objectives, and all China have become a Communist satellite of Moscow by 1930 — but for Chiang Kai-shek. His was the sense of direction, and the strength, which kept the mad milling struggle a Western-oriented *Chinese* revolution instead of a Russia-controlled *Communist* revolution. Which is something the Communists, of course, could never forget nor forgive.

By the time Chiang, after one of his four-month withdraw-

141

als, was insistently called back to head the government at the end of 1927, he had already established this direction for the whole revolutionary movement; and he had made a unified Western-style Republic of China its clearly recognized goal. But he was compelled to fight always vicious and sometimes formidable Communist efforts to destroy both him and his objective, every year and every step of the way. There was always some amount of Communist infiltration and trouble-making inside the Kuomintang itself. There was unceasing Communist destructiveness and sabotage in a country badly needing peace and rehabilitation. And the overall menace, of Communist ambition and intentions with regard to China, hung like a dark cloud over every dream and project. Those factors combined to form a perennial handicap to progress during all of the years from 1928 on, when Chiang was trying so hard to put his government and his country on their feet.

It's true that when the Northern Expedition ended in 1928, and despite the disruptions in that campaign which the Communists had caused, their strength and influence in China reached a very low ebb. Their supreme effort, in Hankow in 1927, to set up a Communist-dominated "Kuo-mintang" government, had been completely defeated. The Soviet's foreign agents had been sent scampering back towards their respective countries. Some ten thousand Communist troops, to which their organized force was reduced, had withdrawn to, and then been driven out of, Nanchang. This "army" had next established itself in Kwangtung Province, made a three-day seizure of Canton which cost fifteen thousand lives and did fifty million dollars property damage, and soon thereafter had been driven, chased, and hunted out of all of Kwangtung like the beasts which they were. And finally the broken remnant of the Chinese Communists had dispersed to the mountainous regions of Kiangsi Province. There, under the gradually more positive dictatorship of Mao Tse-tung, with Chu Teh in

142

military command, and with approximately one thousand revolutionists who had been trained in Moscow universities as the inner core of the organization, they began to rally. Using the most terroristic methods imaginable, they began to seize and consolidate local areas under their "government," and to extend their raids, disorders, and terror into Fukien, Hunan, and Hupeh Provinces.

Chiang Goes After Them . . .

In 1930, during a break in Chiang's long struggle with the warlords, he decided it was time to wipe out this murderous gang. But Mao and his lieutenants had made full use of the opportunity to strengthen their position. They now had nearly a quarter of a million men under arms. They were willing to use means and methods of fighting which Chiang could not consider. The terrain to which they retreated when necessary was almost inaccessible to regular army operations. And Chiang had little surcease from his problem with the "tuchuns." So dislodging the Communists did not prove easy. The 1931 campaign for that purpose was, in the end, a miserable failure. Then came the Japanese invasion of Manchuria, and increasing Japanese aggression, requiring more and more of the Nanking government's troops and attention. Also, in December, 1931 Chiang felt obliged by the political circumstances to withdraw from the government, and did not return until March 7, 1932. It was not until April, 1932 that he could give attention to the Communists again, and they naturally had taken full advantage of this further interlude.

Beginning in 1932 Chiang worked out elaborate methods for organizing local civil volunteer corps, of five hundred men each, under the coordination of provincial authorities, to defend their areas from Communist guerillas; and humanitarian plans for the rehabilitation of captured guerilas who could prove they had been coerced by terror into joining the

Communist ranks. He began to retake the peripheral areas which the Communists had penetrated, to set up the same volunteer system in them, and to squeeze the whole Communist mob into an ever-tightening circle. These efforts were again seriously handicapped in 1933 by the Japanese invasion of Jehol Province; and during Chiang's preoccupation with this critical situation in the North, the Communists routed several of his divisions in Kiangsi before he could return to that front. But during the summer of 1933 Chiang made careful and extensive plans for a fall campaign proportionate to the size and menace of the enemy. For the Communists were now estimated to have five hundred thousand men in their armed forces. Some of these were professional soldiers, but most of them were simple peasants who had been beaten or frightened into fighting for a cause of which they had only the haziest conception.

Communist Atrocities . . .

It is worthwhile to pause at this point long enough to indicate the methods by which the Communists were able to accumulate any such horde, in just four years after fleeing to the Kiangsi mountains. Of course they used all of the ideological arguments and promises of Communism, so far as the Chinese peasants could understand them. But sheer terror was the means on which they really counted. We have no fondness for turning the stomachs of our readers, but the following item from the London *Morning Post,* late in 1932, will probably clarify the Communist procedures as quickly as anything we could offer. It reads:

"The outrages committed by the Red Bandits in several provinces of China during the past few years," states an eye-witness missionary, "are without equal in any age or people, barbarous as they may have been." "All the horrible, most horrible particulars that could be told about this," says an officer of the regular army writing from Kinan in Kiangsi, "would never give a complete idea of the reality;

bodies flayed, hearts torn out, insides scattered about, victims burned alive . . . . not to mention the atrocities against the women. There are not enough words, nor words strong enough, to stigmatize these outrages!" The *Shanghai Journal* is further quoted as giving the record of Communist outrages in Hupeh alone in 1931-32 as "Persons put to death, 164,551; persons disappeared, 946,000; persons kidnapped, 78,000; houses burned, 300,000 . . . ."

It is worth noting, too, that these figures of the *Shanghai Journal,* far from being mere guesses, could have been surprisingly accurate. For the only reason you flay a man, strip off his skin and let him die in horrible agony, instead of shooting him or chopping his head off, is that you want to make widely known to other people what will happen to them if they do not fall in line. And the Chinese Communists have *always* made it a practice to publicize, with names and details, their executions, mass murders, and other atrocities, in order to make terror a more effective weapon in their program.

It is still further worth noting that Mao Tse-tung, the evil genius and unquestioned authority behind these atrocities, was an honored puppet of Moscow, acting under direct orders of Moscow, with the Moscow-trained helpers mentioned above to set the pace in carrying out his commands. And that this was the same government in Moscow which President Roosevelt certainly saved from financial collapse, and probably from political collapse, by official American recognition in 1933, only a few months after this article appeared in the London paper, and right while these outrages in China were actually at their height. This was in reality the far-off beginning of that entanglement of Chiang and of China in the web of our disastrous foreign policy, though the threads and the effect of the entanglement did not begin to show for yet a few more years.

It is finally worth noting, and definitely relevant in a biography of Chiang Kai-shek, that it is this same Mao Tse-tung and the same subordinates who, for the past several years, have been perpetrating equal atrocities on a commensurately wider scale over the whole mainland of China. And it is exactly this same gang whom traitors behind the scenes in our present administration, their gullible dupes out front, and many blind "idealists," are trying so hard to induce us to recognize as a legitimate government today. But that is getting ahead of our story.

The remaining bit of this section of that story is brief. Despite another serious interruption in the form of the Fukien revolt in November, 1933, which revolt the Communists aided, Chiang kept increasing his forces, his drive, and his successes against them. With the result that, by October, 1934, his troops had captured the last Communist "capital" in Kiansi. They then wiped out the few small nests that remained in the province. The Communists were not to be back in that area of China again for fifteen years.

V
AND AGAIN

Unfortunately, they were to be back. But that return is part of a distinct enough division in the whole tragic story to call for a separate chapter — even though it begins chronologically where the last one ended.

As Mao and his fellow Communists saw that they were losing Kiangsi in a complete rout, their guerilla bands began slipping away. The total of these decimated "armies" which were not caught and destroyed, and of the soldiers' families and other non-military personnel migrating with them, amounted to about one hundred thousand men, women, and children. They spread at first into those neighboring provinces where the authority of the national government was weakest, and where petty local warlords could be most easily intimidated. Then they were gradually herded by Mao Tse-tung into several marauding divisions, and started on their famous "Long March" to the Northwest.

Burning, pillaging, diffusing themselves among the very peasants they were robbing and murdering, always fleeing before Chiang Kai-shek's troops but living on the land as they went, these different hordes *flowed* rather than traveled, in a northward direction across the more remote western provinces, for nearly two years. They finally reached Shansi. Driven out of that province, they escaped to the bleak northern regions of Shensi. Here, a thousand miles nearer to the Russian border than any Chinese Communist headquarters had ever been set up before, the remaining fifty thousand of these wandering bandits settled down in the almost inaccessible wastelands. And Mao Tse-tung promptly announced the establishment of the Chinese People's Soviet Republic.

Again, these fifty thousand people formed a hard core of experienced Communists, even more time-and-trouble-tested than those who had fled from Hankow in 1927. They had to depend on brigandage almost entirely in order to live, and the whole purpose of their existence was expansion of their Soviet "government." So terroristic raids into neighboring areas started almost by the time they had squatted in northern Shensi. Soon these raids were spreading into the more populous parts of Shensi, and into the provinces of Ninghsia and Kansu, to the northwest; and even into Shansi again, to the east. To oppose and suppress them, Chiang assigned the Northeastern Army, under Chang Hsueh-liang, and the Shensi provincial army, under Yang Hu-cheng. The Generalissimo was beset with many other difficulties at the time, and this ill-considered dispensation was an almost fatal error. For both Yang and his native Shensi troops proved irresolute in the face of the Communist propaganda and tactics to which they were so closely exposed; while the "Young Marshal's" far more stable and experienced troops wanted to be fighting the Japanese in order to recover their homeland of Manchuria, and were rebellious at the idea of spending their time in fighting the Communists instead. The result of this fermenting situation was the extraordinary Sian Coup d'État of December 12, 1936 — which we now look at from a different angle.

The Sian Coup d'État . . .

Chiang had gone to Lintung, fifteen miles from Sian, for the specific purpose of giving Yang Hu-cheng and the "Young Marshal" his plans and instructions for wiping out the whole Communist establishment once more. He was made a prisoner by these very generals he had come to see. And he was held a prisoner by them, in Sian, until Christmas Day. By that time the "Young Marshal," having through this close contact with Chiang (actually through secretly reading Chiang's diary) arrived at a better understanding of the Generalissimo's policies and of the reasons for them, was deeply repentant. He accompanied Chiang Kai-shek back to Nanking, and there issued one of the most amazing and contrite confessions of guilt in history, sincerely suggesting that any punishment of himself up to the death penalty would be deserved and for the good of the state. The whole life-story of this always earnest and idealistic but unwise and futile man would be a wonderful subject for some novelist's pen. But the net results of this disastrous adventure were tragic for Chiang and for China — as well as for himself. (He is today a retired recluse on the island of Formosa). It hurried the Japanese in their war plans. It seriously damaged Chiang's health for a long time thereafter, through a bad fall and dangerous exposure that occurred during his captivity. It set China back for months in what had been effective and rapid preparations for the approaching war. And, most important of all, it afforded the Communists exactly the period of continued recovery and progress which they needed.

When Japan began all-out war the following August the

Communists were solidly established in their Shensi stronghold, with Yenan as their capital. And under Russia's orders they were making so much noise about their desire to fight the Japanese that Chiang made the final fatal mistake of accepting them and their armies as a part of the Chinese nation for its life-and-death struggle with Japan. The Communists themselves jumped at this opportunity and lied like — well, like Communists — as to how they would behave. Not only were their armies, still unmixed with other troops and still under Communist generals, given the status of National Government forces; but Mao Tse-tung and Chou En-lai and Chu Teh were given high places in the civilian government. Yet as early as October, 1938, only one month after making the most solemn pledges of cooperation, Mao Tse-tung issued a secret directive to his followers that "our policy should be seventy per cent expansion, twenty per cent dealing with the Kuomintang, and ten per cent resisting Japan."

Further along in this same directive Mao said that the Communists should "show our outward obedience to the Central Government . . . but in reality this will serve as camouflage for the existence and development of the party." And a short time later he distributed, to a limited circle of Communist leaders, an explanatory pamphlet which contained such points as these: "Circumstances require a temporary compromise with the Kuomintang . . . It should unmistakably be recognized that armed force is the determining factor in Chinese politics, wherefore we should avail ourselves of the present war to augment our military power so as to form a basis for our struggle for revolutionary leadership in the future."

The Communists Break Loose . . .

Stalin was palpably worried, in 1937, about Japanese advances on the continent of Asia. So the Chinese Communists actually contributed some effective harassing of the

Japanese forces for about two years, though even then they were setting up Communist cells in villages outside of their area, and impressing the peasants of these villages into their armies, all of the time. But after the Stalin-Hitler pact in 1939, and even more completely after the United States entered the war against Japan late in 1941, Stalin's only feeling about the Japanese involvement with China was a desire to keep it going as long as possible. In parallel with this change in Stalin's attitude, the Chinese Communists gradually ceased all pretense of obedience to, or cooperation with, the National Government, or of participation in the war on China's side. They began to devote practically all of their energies to taking advantage of the chaotic war conditions in order to enlarge both their armies and their territorial holdings. Nor did they hesitate to ambush and destroy Chiang's own troops at every opportunity. In Shantung in 1943, just for one illustration, they attacked from the south an army of twenty thousand Nationalists, simultaneously with a Japanese attack from the north, and helped to slaughter the whole force.

One result of this perfidy was that Chiang had to keep large armies, badly needed for fighting the Japanese, actively engaged in preventing the Communists from over-running all of north and central China during the last years of the war. A much more tragic result was the expansion they were still able to accomplish. In 1937 Mao's Communists had been a rabble of guerillas in the sandlands of northern Shensi. They came out of the war, in 1945, in control of provinces containing a population of ninety million people; and with a party membership of one million, half of them under arms, to enforce that control. All of this, as George Creel wrote, had been accomplished "while the energies and resources of Chiang Kai-shek were being devoted to the life-and-death struggle against the Japanese."

And We Help Them . . .

The history of the next five years in China has now been recorded so many times that we'll forego repeating it here, except in broadest outline. It is not a story that any honorable American can write, or read, without a feeling of shame, anger, and regret. Chiang Kai-shek and China itself were completely exhausted after fighting overwhelming Japanese invasion forces for many long years. Chiang and his countrymen needed and *deserved* the help of America more than have any other leader and his people, at any time in the 170 years since we ourselves became a nation. Instead, he found the American government deserting him, deceiving him, betraying him, and aiding the Chinese Communists at every turn to take over his country. In fact it took long-continued, extensive, and powerful influence on the part of our government, exerted against Chiang and for his enemies, to enable the Communists to win; and that influence was the decisive factor in bringing about the final results.

There are readers, long blinded by the pro-Communist propaganda which was an adjunct of that very influence, who simply have not been willing to face the clear historical record of the period, and who will consider the above sentences as exaggerations. For corroboration that these are statements of plain unvarnished fact, we refer such readers to the testimony of those very Americans of the most unquestioned standing who were the closest participants in, and observers of, the events in question: General Claire Chennault, General George E. Stratemeyer, General Albert C. Wedemeyer, Ambassador Patrick J. Hurley, and many more. For readers who wish more details and more exposition, there are books by George Creel and Freda Utley and William Henry Chamberlin and George Moorad and Elizabeth Brown — and the recent full-scale biography of Patrick Hurley by Don Lohbeck. These and

151

many other careful writers have put down, for all to see who really wish to do so, the almost incredible record of desertion and betrayal — and the huge part played therein by treason within our government — with incontrovertible documentation.

In these books you will find the official record of the secret betrayal of Chiang Kai-shek at Yalta which was so far-reaching and so shameless that President Roosevelt categorically lied about it to the American Congress (although he may have been too sick by then to know what he was doing or what he had done); that neither Chiang Kai-shek nor even our ambassador to China was given any inkling of it until months afterward; and that the American people were not allowed to know anything about it until more than a year later. You will learn how George Marshall used the power of the American Government to harass Chiang Kai-shek and to save the Communists from annihilation time after time — and of his gloating boast that "with a stroke of the pen" he had disarmed thirty-nine of Chiang's anti-Communist divisions. You will learn of the deliberate death blow given to Chiang's last hopes of saving his country by the publication of our State Department's infamously slanted "White Paper." And you will learn of a thousand other items, large and small, in the sorry story, which we have promised not to redeploy here.

We ourselves have tried in two small books, *May God Forgive Us* and *The Life Of John Birch*, to cast some light on the combination of treason, misguided idealism, and stupidity, which brought about our gift of the Chinese mainland to agents of the Kremlin. But we have studied the documents and records and actions far more now than when those books were written. And we are firmly convinced today that, with regard to the actual treason involved in the story of those five years, not even the half has ever been told. The greatest of all the obstacles Chiang Kai-shek had faced, on his road to the creation of a unified republican China, was the Communist terror. We helped immeasurably to convert that obstacle into a moving, offensive juggernaut which pushed Chiang himself into the sea. Not only did we, by our help to Mao and our harm to Chiang, hand to the Communists this greatest of all their victories since they took over Russia itself; but this gift was planned and accomplished by traitors within our government, many of whom we believe to be still there, and still more powerful, today. And this estimate, too, is entirely relevant, in the continuing life-story of Chiang Kai-shek.

VI
THE BIRTH OF A NATION

Even with the whole mainland gone, however, Chiang and the Republic of China did not simply disappear, as the Communists expected. It is a truism worthy of frequent repetition that, with such a leader dedicated so completely to so epic a cause, all is not lost so long as he still draws breath. With brilliant foresight, never flagging determination, and the resourcefulness of genius, Chiang saved out of apparently complete defeat the one chance of ultimate victory. Before the Communists were aware of what was happening, or could then do anything about it, he established both himself and his government on the island of Taiwan, and made that ancient Chinese province the *temporary* headquarters of the Republic.

There, since 1950, while prevented by us from retaking the offensive against the Communists, Chiang has had the opportunity of concentrating more attention than ever before on the problem of Chinese self-government – the one other great obstacle to his lifetime aim. It is a problem which he has fully recognized, and tackled with all of the energy he could ever spare from other more urgent difficulties, for thirty years. The basic plan of the Chinese Revolution, which plan Chiang inherited from Dr. Sun Yat-sen and to which he

153

has given unswerving allegiance ever since, envisioned three distinct stages: (1) The overthrow of the Manchu dynasty and suppression of all counter-revolutionaries by a military government; (2) then a period of political "tutelage," when the Kuomintang would act as trustees of the Chinese people, while helping them as rapidly as possible to overcome their complete inexperience with political affairs and "democratic" processes; and (3) the adoption of a constitution, with universal suffrage and free elections, and with the Kuomintang sinking into its proper relationship with other political parties.

The most amazing thing about this farsighted plan, so appropriate for China, is that it was not a fraudulent piece of lip service to a dream-world idea — as have been so many similar promises for the future advanced by ambitious revolutionary leaders for the sake of present power. Dr. Sun really meant it. So did his closest followers. And Chiang Kai-shek has done everything he could to carry out that program, faithfully and honorably, at every stage. He has done so despite many appealing temptations to make of himself a dictator for the sake of a dictator's efficiency, and in the face of difficulties more tremendous than Dr. Sun could ever have foreseen.

As far back as 1928, as soon as the Northern Expedition was successfully completed, Chiang took steps to advance the revolutionary organization from the first stage listed above to the second; from the period of purely military government to that of political tutelage under the guidance and leadership of the Kuomintang. He submitted a proposal for an Organic Law, which was approved by the Fifth Plenary Session of the Central Executive Committee of the Kuomintang on October 4, 1928. This Organic Law provided for a Government with five branches, or yuans: An Executive Yuan, a Legislative Yuan, a Control Yuan, a Judicial Yuan, and an Examination (or Civil Service) Yuan.

The five-pronged pattern of civil administration had deep roots in the customs of the country, and thus gave the new republican order some degree of continuity with Chinese governmental traditions. During the period of tutelage there was to be a State Council of from twelve to sixteen members, which were to include the presidents of each of the five yuans. And the president of this State Council was the actual head of the government.

Then, in 1930, over strong protests of many of the leaders of the Kuomintang, Chiang succeeded in having its Central Executive Committee arrange for a People's Convention. It opened in Nanking on May 5, 1931. The 447 delegates had been elected by farmers' associations, labor unions, chambers of commerce and other businessmen's associations, educational and professional associations, and the Kuomintang itself. It was as broadly representative of the Chinese people as was possible under the circumstances. This convention discussed and debated the outstanding national problems, and passed many resolutions looking toward their solution. The delegates also adopted a Provisional Constitution, which was largely a confirmation of the Organic Law, to be effective until the end of the tutelage period. At the time it was hoped and expected that, by 1935 at the latest, a completely representative People's Convention, actually elected by popular vote, could be assembled. That convention was to provide for regular elections and normal republican procedures and to mark the move out of "tutelage" to the third and final stage of truly republican government. But these expectations were doomed to long disappointment. Because of the continuous struggle with the Communists and then with the Japanese invasion, China was ruled under the Organic Law of 1928 for twenty years. And Chiang's power during all of that time always depended on his standing with, and the support of, the Central Executive Committee of the Kuomintang.

Domestic Progress . . .

Even more important, however, than this fidelity on Chiang's part to the fundamental ideal and purpose of the Chinese Revolution, was the domestic progress under his leadership from the end of the Northern Campaign in 1928 to the Japanese attack on Shanghai in 1937. Despite such unceasing trouble and so many handicaps, there was remarkable progress toward the achievement of responsible government in actual practice, and toward the economic and cultural improvement of the lives of the Chinese people. During every peaceful interlude, and to the fullest extent possible even while he was fighting warlords, Communists, or Japanese invaders, Chiang put brilliant inspiration, unexcelled organizing ability, and unending work into the non-military requirements for building a modern, prosperous, unified, independent, well-governed Republic of China.

There is no room in this paper to catalogue the highways built in a country where there had been only mule paths outside of the large cities; the thousands of miles of railroad added to the primitive original system; the exploration and commercial development of mineral resources; the rural rehabilitation; the tremendous improvement in banking facilities; and all of the parts and pieces of this economic improvement that was carried on while the sound of gunfire was never long absent nor far away. But it is worth taking the space to itemize the program which was set before the Chinese people in 1935 as their goal:

1. To develop all natural resources along modern lines.
2. To modernize agricultural methods.
3. To increase the production of raw materials.
4. To establish new industries to manufacture and process the nation's raw materials.
5. To extend the nation's communications, including railways, highways, and airlines.
6. To undertake vigorously forestation and river control.

7. To guarantee protection to all who invest their money in productive enterprises.

8. To provide measures for the harmonious cooperation of capital and labor.

9. To encourage investment of hoarded capital.

10. To simplify the currency.

11. To place taxation on a scientific basis.

This was no Communist five-year plan, full of statistical quotas of guns and butter to be achieved by state-managed enterprises; toward the filling of which quotas semi-slave labor was to be driven and goaded, or stimulated by propaganda as race horses are "doped up" by hypodermic injections. This outline set no tasks, and provided no measuring rods as bases for collective punishments or rewards. It was a common-sense analysis of China's needs and opportunities, converted into a constructive guidance chart for a people just beginning to emerge from a backward and preponderantly agricultural economy. It was offered as a permanent program in which free individuals, because of the incentives offered in a free economy to improve their own individual lots — by undertakings, risks, and labors of their own choice — would automatically improve the standard of living of the whole nation by their cumulative efforts. It contemplated a certain amount of government planning and subsidization in connection with some of the objectives listed, but leaned very heavily on the inducements of free enterprise, and on the maintenance of a political climate in which free enterprise could prosper. And it is very much worth taking the space to point out that an amazing amount of this program was translated into action during so brief a period before the Japanese invasion began.

Chiang never had the chance to bring to completion that organization of provincial governments, and local *hsien* or county governments within the provinces, which he so hopefully started, and to which local administrative bodies,

157

closer to the citizens, he counted on turning over so many of the functions necessarily performed during the tutelage period by the central government. And yet John K. Fairbank, whose bias in favor of Chiang's enemies can be most easily illustrated by the fact that in the 367 pages of his book on *The United States and China* he never once tells or implies that the Chinese Communists ever committed a single atrocity – Prof. Fairbank has written that "the National Government of China at Nanking in the decade from 1927 to 1937 was the most modern and effective that China had known." This was a conclusion that no historian could escape or deny without ruining his reputation as a historian. It was also as *good* a government and as honest a government as it was possible for Chiang to make it, under the circumstances and with the personnel on which he had to depend.

Nor was he willing to leave any facet of Chinese weakness, nor any room for improvement, untouched. He worked for years on the humiliating concessions to foreign governments, the so-called "Unequal Treaties," which involved foreign control over Chinese territory, tariffs, customs, and trade. And he finally succeeded in getting all such treaties peacefully abrogated in 1942.

He early recognized the need for the emotional appeal of a more ethical, more sanitary, more humane, more civilized life among the Chinese masses. And the New Left movement which he inaugurated and inspired in 1934 had a tremendous influence on the trend of Chinese thinking and character during so disturbed a transition period from the old to the new as China was undergoing. A devout and true Christian himself, Chiang did his utmost, by example and by organized instruction, to inculcate into the Chinese people the best of the Christian virtues, morals, and attitudes without any loss of disparagement of the great traditions of family solidarity and industriousness inherited from their own past. With any breaks in any similar situation in history, Chiang would, we believe, long ago have converted and molded China into a nation of which he and his countrymen could be very proud. With all of his thirty-year efforts destroyed by evil forces of a nature and magnitude entirely beyond his control, he has now set out to rebuild patiently and skillfully again towards the same objective.

VII
THE REPUBLIC OF CHINA

So far as the form and spirit of the official government of China is concerned, Chiang succeeded in reaching the third and final stage of Dr. Sun Yat-sen's plan before the mainland was lost. Immediately after the war, and regardless of both the military and political difficulties unendingly raised by the Communists, Chiang pushed towards this goal as rapidly and as vigorously as he could. A National Assembly met on November 15, 1946, to consider a permanent constitution for China which had been worked out by a very able Political Consultative Conference. This constitution, consisting of 14 chapters and 175 articles, was approved on December 25, 1946, to go into effect on December 25, 1947.

In tune with world-wide post-war "democratic" thinking, this new charter provided for a social insurance system; for government limitation on, as well as protection of, private property; for government management of public utilities; and for many other "progressive" features which have no place in the classical functions of a republican government. But these features certainly were more justified by the circumstances in China in 1946 than in the United States of the 1930's — from which they were largely copied. And offsetting these tendencies of the new government to reach too far into the private lives of its citizens, and to assume too much responsibility for their welfare, were the most complete safeguards against tyranny that modern constitutional experience could devise. The "bill of rights" clauses spelled out a comprehensive guarantee of personal liberties and rights, including a *habeas corpus* provision, and made the government responsible for the illegal acts of its officials and agents.

In accordance with this constitution the first nation-wide election in China's history was held on November 21 to 23, 1947. On March 29, 1948, the 1,744 delegates elected in November convened as a National Assembly. Their most important business was the election of a president and vice president. Chiang felt that there would be strong psychological advantages for the new republic if it started off with some chief executive other than himself, and preferably with one who was even independent of the Kuomintang. He made an announcement that he was not a candidate for the presidency, in which he tried to make this point of view clear; and in which he also assured the delegates that he would be willing to serve the nation to the best of his ability in any capacity under the new president. But neither the nation nor the delegates would allow this withdrawal, and Chiang was elected for the six-year term by a vote ratio of approximately seven to one.

The fact that there was plenty of room for the development and display of widely varied opinions and purposes within the new governmental framework, however, soon became obvious. There was a vigorous contest for the vice-presidency. Sun Fo, despite the support of the "old guard" of the Kuomintang, and the fact that Chiang himself was believed to favor Sun's candidacy, lost out in a close election to Li Tsung-jen, the old Kwangsi warlord now acting as a leader of the "liberals". And dissensions over many matters became more visible and more acrimonious when the first Legislative Yuan met a few weeks later. Chiang and his Kuomintang associates, true to their trusteeship, had now given China a parliamentary republican government, with all of its blessings and all of its encumbrances, for better or for worse.

Although this fidelity to promises and to ideals was praiseworthy, the Communist push for all of China was already so far advanced that, in retrospect, its wisdom may be doubted. The Communist build-up was so rapid, their methods so pernicious, and the anti-Chiang pro-Communist influence and actions of the American government and its representatives so decisive, that on January 1, 1949, Chiang stepped aside. Without upsetting the whole constitutional and political situation at so crucial a stage by resigning the presidency, he simply removed himself in favor of the vice president. This withdrawal was to give Vice President Li Tsung-jen and the Kwangsi leaders a chance to try out *their* way of stopping the Communists by negotiations and appeasement, for which Li and some of the Americans had been clamoring. And because Li Tsung-jen was widely supposed to be more favored by, and hence able to get more help from, the American government, Chiang insisted that Li remain as Acting President even when, three months later, he himself came back into the government to be of whatever help he could.

By early 1950, however, the debacle of all Li's plans was so complete and the demand for Chiang's resumption of leadership so insistent that, on March 31 — on the unanimous petition of the 331 members present at a meeting of the Legislative Yuan — Chiang again took on the full duties and title of the presidency. Li Tsung-jen, having made an unearthly mess of everything, had fled to America "for his health" and "for more aid." Chiang, having already made as careful plans and preparations as were possible under the circumstances, saved what little he could out of the almost complete ruin, for movement to, and a new stand on, the island of Taiwan. And in 1954, when the next elections were held in a Republic of China now reduced territorially to this one province, Chiang was re-elected for another six-year term.

On Taiwan . . .

So, from the very beginning of his great rebuilding task on that island, Chiang has had the completely constitutional government which he had so long visualized for all of China. And although there have still been many other problems and worries, and many obstacles — with the twin threats, of Communist invasion, and of diplomatic betrayal by the other governments of the free world, always hanging like dark clouds overhead — Chiang and some very devoted followers have been making that constitutional government work with a success that has astounded both his friends and his enemies. They have profited as far as possible from the mistakes of the past. They have been well aware of the importance of what they were doing, through its effect on world opinion, not only in its direct relationship to the future of China, but in the whole world-wide fight against Communism of which the battle in China is a part. And, with rare exceptions, they have not only benefitted from excellent teamwork among themselves, but have had the increasingly whole-hearted support of the Taiwanese provincial population. President Chiang Kai-shek and Madame Chiang and Vice-President Chen Cheng and Prime Minister O.K. Yui and Foreign Minister George Yeh and too many other able and loyal associates to be named here — most of them tested and proved by many long years of unending struggle together for the same goal — have created in Taiwan the kind of government they wanted to create on the mainland of China, and will yet create there if they have the opportunity. And it is not just this writer's opinion, but that of almost every competent observer who has visited Taiwan and studied their accomplishments, that they are offering, for the whole world to see, the best government that any part of Asia, and certainly any part of East Asia, has ever had.

VIII
A MODEL FOR ASIA

Nor is it a passive government, but a very active one, in dealing with and trying to solve the numberless problems which all the strange circumstances of time and place have put before it. One particular policy may serve as a small sample to illustrate a great whole of such activities. For, as David N. Rowe, Professor of Political Science at Yale, pointed out on his recent return from two years in Taiwan: "Free China is the only place in Asia today where a genuine and farreaching agrarian reform has been put into effect by an Asian Government on its own initiative, without bloodshed and violence . . . ."

The Chinese Communists were largely "sold" to the American public, during the fatal years when they were wrecking China as a nation and then taking it over, as "agrarian reformers." This characterization was a subtle and deliberate lie on the part of the traitors and fellow travelers who spread it, on two counts. First, China has never had the legal requirement nor even the custom of primogeniture. On the death of the father his land was invariably divided equally among all of his sons. This automatically kept land holdings, with very few exceptions, quite small. So there simply were no large estates in land, or large farms, to be split up by the Communists. But because China was so little industrialized, the usual Communist slogans and formulas for stirring up hatred of employees against employers did not have enough matrices in which to work. After many bitter arguments between Mao's bosses in Moscow, he was allowed and helped to give Marxism a new twist, adapted to the agricultural economy of China. For the proletarian cry of "workers of the world unite," he substituted an appeal to the poorest peasants and tenant-farmers to rise in murderous hatred against all of their neighbors who owned a few acres of land.

Only in that way was Mao able to find a large enough class of people in China in whom there was any chance of sowing discontent from which to reap the whirlwind that he wanted. And second, when the Communists did take over an area and seize the small farms of a few acres each from the thrifty owners, they did not parcel these acres out to the tenants or other peasants, but followed exactly the opposite practice of collectivizing them under state ownership.

Nevertheless, the tremendous propaganda effect of the mere phrase, "agrarian reform," had by 1950 reached such proportions that it had permeated the thinking of everybody in Asia, and its value to the Communists could not be ignored. So Chiang and his associates early determined to put through "agrarian reform" on Taiwan; but on a basis that would be fair and sensible and well thought out, from the point of view of everybody concerned.

Real Agrarian Reform . . .

Their first job was to obtain a satisfactory degree of willing cooperation from the landlords and farm owners. And although one member of the administrative team later compared this undertaking to negotiating with a tiger for his fur, the government had two powerful arguments for gaining the consent it wanted. First, the negotiators pointed out that, if the Communists ultimately succeeded in taking Taiwan, *as could happen*, the best anybody who might be called a landlord could expect, besides having his land seized, was to have his hands and feet chopped off. This was not only perfectly true, but there were plenty of refugees on Taiwan who could vouch for its truth from their own observations on the mainland. (A few years ago an American doctor, who had remained behind the Communist lines for a few months when they swept over north China and had later succeeded in getting out, gave in the *Saturday Evening Post* some details of the Communists' treatment of "landlords", from his own firsthand experiences.) The second argument, entirely on the positive side, was that the government would relieve these landowners of the onus and danger of being "landlords" by arranging for the sale of their farms to the tenants on fair terms, at a fair price to be determined by local committees of landlords and tenants together.

It was then settled that tenants were to be enabled to buy and pay for their two to three acres each, by giving them ten years to make the payments, in semi-annual installments, out of what they could earn on these small plots. Next, both to be fair to the "landlords", so that they would not be paid the later installments in money which had become worth far less than when the sale was made — an honest admission by the government that it could never be sure of preventing inflation under all of the difficulties it faced — and because payment "in kind" would be so much easier for the new peasant owners, it was arranged that all such semi-annual installments were to be paid in given quantities of rice.

Finally, two other strong considerations were taken care of in the same plan. In the first place, these "landlords" were likely to be among the most able and thrifty citizens on Taiwan, whose industry and intelligence and desire "to get ahead" were badly needed in helping to lift the economy of the whole island to a higher level. In the second place, there was nothing the island needed so much as industrialization, beginning especially with small cement-block plants and a hundred similar infant industries geared to the close and immediate requirements of the people. And who would have the skill and ambition to build up these local industries in each community more surely than the former "landlords"? So the arrangement finally worked out that the government would act as an intermediary business agent in these deals; that the semi-annual payments of rice by the new peasant-owners, for the whole purchase price, would be made to the government; that proportionate installments of seventy per cent of the purchase price would simultaneously be paid by the government to the former landlords, in rice or its current money equivalent; and that thirty per cent of the original purchase price would be given to the landlords, at the time of the original sale, in shares in these new industrial enterprises — for which the government would itself be repaid by the remaining thirty per cent of the rice installments from the new farm owners.

It was an excellent program, to fit unusual conditions; and one for which, in all honesty, the Joint Commission on Rural Reconstruction, which American aid and agents have helped to establish and run, must be given its full share of the credit. Not even the most vigorous critic of our whole incredibly wasteful and harmful foreign-aid program can claim that there has been no good in it anywhere. The operation of the Joint Commission has been one of those happy exceptions; for in this instance our money — very little money, which was probably an advantage — and effort have been used, with the encouragement and assistance of a native government, directly to help its people to become more prosperous, instead of to help that government to become more powerful.

This writer personally has been present, visiting a former Chinese tenant-farmer, now the proud owner of his 2½ acres, on the dirt floor of the one main room in his cottage in the middle of his small irrigated field, when the bill for his semi-annual rice payment arrived. He had the rice, was going to be able to make the payment, and not only he and his wife and daughter — the daughter sitting on the floor busily weaving straw into coarse hats, for sale at prices which would give her a few cents per day for her labor — were happy about it; but even the one water buffalo wallowing in the hole outside seemed to be happy. And we felt reasonably sure that the former "landlord," who had perhaps owned four plots this size, or ten acres altogether, was happy over the whole deal as well.

And Prosperity . . .

Under this program during the past four years, and a similarly enlightened program for the sale of public land, nearly seventy-five percent of the farm area of Taiwan has now become owner-cultivated. And the beneficial results, combined with the results of other equally careful combinations of government guidance and individual incentive, can legitimately be described as stupendous. The annual rice crop prior to 1950 had been about 1,200,000 tons. By 1955 it had climbed to approximately 1,600,000 tons; and for 1956 the total was over 1,850,000 tons. The only reason the sugar crop has not grown in a similar proportion is that it is limited by international agreements to around 700,000 tons per year. The hog population has more than doubled since 1949. And the production of other foodstuffs is rapidly increasing.

There were from five to six million people on Taiwan before Chiang Kai-shek, and then the great stream of refugees arrived. Today there are more than nine million, and "Formosa" is the second most densely populated "country" in the world. But there is no starvation nor even serious malnutrition anywhere, which is of itself rare in Asia. "To understand what has happened," wrote John C. Caldwell last summer, "it is necessary to take a trip over the island. A couple of days ago I drove down to Taichung, in the central part. (I'd made this same trip two years ago.) In no country in Asia have I seen such evidence of rural prosperity. Everywhere new farm houses are being built. The fields were lush with bumper crops. In each town there was evidence of healthy growth in small industry. In three hundred miles of traveling I did not see a single beggar. Yet in Tokyo, one afternoon, I counted an even dozen within three blocks of the Imperial Hotel."

But progress in agriculture has been attended by equal

167

progress in education (especially vocational training), in industry, and in other areas of human activity, which we do not have room to illustrate at length. Also writing from Taiwan last summer, Mr. Henry R. Lieberman of the *New York Times* reported, for instance, that there has been "an across-the-board increase of about one hundred percent in industrial output compared with 1950. Pointing to electrical power as a gauge of industrial growth, American engineers here note that the present 'peaking' capacity is around 350,000 kilowatts as against 150,000 to 170,000 kilowatts during pre-1945 Japanese rule." And Mr. A.T. Steele, of the *New York Herald-Tribune,* wrote from Taipei last October 8: "Amid the noisy publicity being given to the grandiose five-year plans of other Asian countries, scant attention has been paid to the very real industrial progress on Formosa by Nationalist China . . . . Formosa now is turning out an expanding list of industrial products, including textiles, electric fans, bicycles, electric motors, cables, aluminum war and other goods." Mr. Steele further points out that, despite the huge increase in population, the living standard of the people of Formosa has improved steadily since the termination of the war.

The food and the sanitation in most of the 250 restaurants in the city of Taipei are not of a sort to tempt the American visitor; and the general living conditions, compared to those we are accustomed to, are extremely low. But compared, as they should be, with general living conditions in India or Hongkong or almost anywhere else in Asia, they are very good indeed, with the promise of becoming better all of the time. This relative gain in a material standard of living, however, is only one part of the achievement of the Nationalist government, and of the contrast with conditions on the mainland. On Taiwan there is complete freedom of movement for everybody. Practically the only policemen you ever see are engaged in directing traffic, which consists mainly of a few automobiles surrounded and impeded by thousands of the bustling man-pedalled three-wheel pedicab taxis. Ownership and protection of all private property is assured. There is freedom of speech, freedom of worship, a free press, and a feeling of freedom in the air that is taken for granted.

It is not possible, of course, for the people of Taiwan actually to shout about their good fortune across the hundred miles of choppy ocean, so as to be heard on the mainland. But from the island of Quemoy, near the coast, which the Nationalists still hold, it sometimes is. And the lonely but hardworking and patriotic young Chinese, on that dangerously fortified island, love to do so. "I've got plenty of rice to eat, trousers to wear, and a Parker fountain pen — what have you got?" is their favorite taunt to the Communists on the other side of the narrow strip of water. A fountain pen, you quickly discover in Taipei, and especially a well-known American fountain pen, is a badge of prosperity, literacy, and ambition; and fully half of all the many stores in downtown Taipei display a counter of fountain pens, no matter what other goods they sell. It makes an excellent symbol of the opportunity and the outlook on Taiwan, in comparison with the mainland, as those who live in Chiang's Republic of China are well aware. It is ardently to be hoped, for the sake of the long-suffering Chinese people, and for the great gain of the whole remaining free world in its struggle against the Communist tyranny, that Chiang Kai-shek will yet live to see that symbol freely sold in every village of a Republic of China which exercises peaceful rule over all of its thirty-five provinces and its five hundred million people.

IX
LOOK HOMEWARD, ANGEL

As gratifying in themselves as may be the happy accomplishments on Taiwan, however, they are still more important to Chiang and his followers as means to a greater end. The hearts of these men are still on the mainland. Their memories and much of their present thoughts are with their now enslaved and tortured comrades, kindred, and fellow-patriots in Chungking, Canton, Peiping, and Nanking. Their unceasing ambition remains what it has been, throughout decades of struggle, suffering and vicissitude: to make a unified republican nation out of all of China. Any biographical sketch of Chiang Kai-shek which simply left him happily governing the increasingly prosperous, self-sufficient, and model province of Taiwan would be grossly lacking in both insight and completeness. For Chiang himself emphatically does not accept any such conclusion to his lifetime of untiring effort. Nor do those around him. When this writer said goodbye to Madame Chiang, at her mountain home above Taipei, his last remark was: "The next time I come to see you, I hope it will be in . . . . " The pause posed a question as to which city on the mainland should be named. "In Peiping," she replied, with a smile, but without hesitation.

The Communists have pulled every stop in their propaganda organ to persuade the West, and especially the American public, that Chiang is now "passé," that his cause is lost, and that his hope of a return to the mainland is only a futile and forlorn dream. But the Communists themselves know better. It is exactly because they do know better that they and their sympathizers try so hard to discount the possibility into nothingness.

For, while all Communist regimes depend on terror as a means of staying in power, the Chinese Communists have had to depend on it more continuously and completely than any other. They have now killed or sent to slave labor camps approximately one out of every ten persons in the whole population. So there is no family and no non-Communist individual on the mainland of China who has not known Communist terror close at home. How much resistance and sabotage the Communists have to face can be indicated by the report of Lo Jui-ching, Mao's "Minister of Public Security," to the Communist "People's Congress" last summer. He revealed that in the last six years there have been 5,549,030 cases of "counter-revolution" on the mainland. This is almost one million "incidents" per year. These figures have to be sifted a bit, in the light of other information, to arrive at any enumeration of sizable uprisings. But even then the most conservative figures should shock our collective American conscience out of some of its complacency. The hatred of Mao's gang is so intense and so widespread, over all the huge area and among the five hundred million tightly enslaved people, that there are today and for a long time have been *an average of seven hundred revolts per day* in China. The whole country is a seething cauldron, kept from exploding by the ruthless suppresson of a merciless police state.

The Rule Of One Percent . . .

Without going into the starvation and economic stagnation which underlie the building of dams, railroad building, and other purposely spectacular products of forced labor extravagantly concentrated on a few such jobs, there is another factor of great weakness in the Chinese Communist position. This is the tenuousness of their organizational control over so vast a number of bitter subjects. It is by the incredible brutality and cruelty of their terroristic suppression, rather than by the numers behind it, that they keep such a population subdued. At the Eighth Chinese Communist Party Congress in Peiping in September, 1956 (which was attended by Communists from fifty-nine nations!), there were 1,021 delegates representing the 10,734,384 Chinese Communists which the party claimed to have as members. This, it should be noted, is only a little more than two percent of the population of the mainland, and there is

171

reason to believe that these figures are highly inflated. The Communists have proved that with from three to five percent of the people of any country as a tightly disciplined core of control, they can keep all the people of that country in perpetual subjection. But from one source of knowledge and information concerning Communist China, in which we have great confidence, we receive an emphatic estimate that Mao does not have more than one percent of that population behind him. And even at the most discouraging guess we can make, his support is dangerously thin.

Aware of this vulnerability, biding his time until he can take advantage of it, stands Chiang Kai-shek. The threat to the Communists is constant and frightening. For here is available, as the leader of the liberation forces in China, a man who is well-known to all of its people, even the most illiterate peasants, as a great historical figure; and who has been identified as a vigorous and unswerving opponent of Communism in the minds of these people for more than thirty years. There is no such leader, with comparable prestige and equal personal following, to head up a revolt in any other satellite nation. Those courageous patriots who would be willing to brave the terror would know that they could count on leadership which was able, experienced, and which would not betray them. Once it became known that Chiang Kai-shek had landed on the mainland of China, with enough military force to protect himself from immediate capture and to serve as a nucleus for those rallying to his standard, the seven hundred daily uprisings of futile despair, which now take place, would mushroom and merge into effective and confident rebellion. The spirit of revolt would sweep the whole country, province after province, like a prairie fire. And not only would Mao and Chu Teh and Chou En-lai be unable to stop it; the Russians themselves do not have enough strength, in men or tanks or planes or even in atom bombs, to put out such a conflagration, once it got well under way, before so many similar fires, starting and spreading in other satellites, would sweep away their whole slave empire.

But the Russians do have enough diplomatic strength, and influence over our government, to see that we keep Chiang and his now powerful army bottled up on Taiwan. He cannot transport enough men and arms across the Formosa Strait, to establish even a beachhead, without our consent and against the guns of our Seventh Fleet. The fate of Chiang and of China is still inextricably entangled in the web of American foreign policy, as it has been for twenty years. And no matter how many specious explanations or high-sounding phrases our government spokesmen advance to account for the incredible waverings and gyrations of that policy, there is only one motivating principle at the core of this forensic exhibition which they really expect to make sense to the American people. The only even plausible justification of our current absurd course is — when stripped of all its persiflage — that we are afraid of Russia. So we had rather mark time, steadily appease the Communists, see our friends massacred as in East Germany and Hungary, lose our allies one by one, wait for the Russians to attack us whenever *they* are ready, and then fight the Communists in the streets of our home towns instead of letting Chiang fight them for us in the mountains of Chekiang.

A Look At The Score . . .

A few hundred Communists started from scratch, in what was then Petrograd, in 1917. Even by 1945 the international Communist conspiracy actually controlled only Russia, the Russia-absorbed states of Latvia, Esthonia, and Lithuania, about one-third of Poland, and an uncertain part of a few provinces in the north of China. Today this conspiracy rules Russia, all of Poland, Albania, Yugoslavia, Roumania, Bulgaria, Hungary, Czechoslovakia, East Germany, Mongolia, Manchuria, all of China except Taiwan Province, North Korea, North Vietnam,

173

and Tibet. It also now controls the governments, if not yet the peoples, of Indonesia, Burma, India, Ceylon, Afghanistan, Syria, and Egypt. It has infiltrated its agents into almost all the governments of the world, to the extent that it now exercises some degree of influence over each of them and a huge degree of influence over many. Year by year and almost month by month, despite all of our pretenses about "containment" or "controlling aggression," the Iron Curtain is lowered over more of the earth's surface, and more millions of the earth's peoples are made slaves of the Kremlin tyrants. How long is this to go on?

One thing is certain. If we always and everywhere fight only a defensive and delaying action, we must ultimately come to the point where there is no more ground to lose. Our only possible chance of salvation is to start, sometime, somewhere, recovering some of the ground already lost. The place to begin *rolling back the curtain*, we believe, is across the Formosa Strait. We believe that taking such iniative is the one best and surest way *to prevent* World War III and the atomic devastation it would bring. Let Chiang Kai-shek start giving the Kremlin gang their hands full in Eastern Asia. They couldn't ignore the explosion, because they know his success would blow up their whole system. And they certainly would not start dropping bombs on the United States, to thus mobilize all our strength actively against them, while trying to subdue such serious trouble on their flank. We believe that this method of attacking the Soviet, obliquely and by reversing their own strategy on them, is the one imaginable military action which they really fear. The very possibility of such action accounts for the subtlety, the extensiveness, and the vigor of their now stepped-up efforts to discredit and supplant Chiang Kai-shek on almost any terms.

X
A BRIEF APPRAISAL

By our system of reckoning ages, Chiang Kai-shek will be

seventy years old this coming October. In appearance he could easily pass for sixty; by his physical and mental vigor he would be taken for fifty or fifty-five. There is no slightest sign of senility in anything he thinks, says, or does. Except for the injury suffered during his Sian captivity, he has never undergone any serious illness. Especially during the last thirty years he has led an abstemious, carefully self-disciplined life, with moderation as its watchword and work as the only excess to which he has ever yielded. Nor is he the kind to be sent to an early grave by ulcerous reactions to his many problems. He has always been able to take fortune and misfortune in his stride, without letting either ruin him. Against misfortune, in particular, he has two ample defenses which stave off lasting ill effects, either physical or mental. The first is a lifelong habit, after going through a severe crisis, of retiring to some mountain retreat for rest and meditation — from which he always returns with renewed strength and determination. The second is his fervent Christianity. Since 1928 his steadily deepening faith has helped to sustain his courage through trials and troubles that sometimes seemed to fall like a never-ending hailstorm. This faith has kept alive his hope after defeats that seemed final and irreversible. It has enabled him to face with calm fortitude all the tragic surprises of a life that has overlapped two eras and merged them together. And as a result of these habits, traits of character, and this mental steadfastness, it seems happily probable that, barring assassination or accident, Chiang Kai-shek will still be able to lead the fight for his dream of a unified Republic of China for many years to come.

While Chiang may find great comfort in his religion, however, he has never found in it any excuse for accepting the accomplishments of Satanic men as beyond his power or responsibility to combat. He could easily claim as the guiding principle of his own life the majestically simple reconciliation of Laurence Clifton Jones: "I have always prayed as if it was all up to the Lord, and worked as if it was all up to me." And

175

having an extremely practical mind, Chiang has approached each task with the feeling that it was his duty to outwork, outthink, outmaneuver, and if necessary outfight, whatever forces of evil might be arrayed against him. This practicality of his outlook, and the vigor of action to which it leads, form the basis for a revealing characterization of Chiang given this writer by an American officer who served in a liaison capacity with the Nationalist armies during World War II. "Oh, Chiang Kai-shek is a Christian all right," he said. "But he's no cream puff, and don't you forget it!"

A Leader, Not a Driver . . .

Chiang is in all respects a leader of men, and not a driver. He likes to carry his followers along by example, and to win his way by persuasion, whenever possible. By nature he shuns the more direct and efficient methods of dictatorship, and prefers the more arduous and frustrating, but ultimately more satisfactory, procedures of negotiation and of parliamentary deliberations. Because of his background and thorough military training, this attitude may have been achieved and self-imposed at the cost of considerable internal struggle and self-discipline; but his devotion to the goal of a modern republican government for China made such genuine "republicanism" imperative in the leader of the movement, and Chiang has lived up to every requirement of the theme, in spirit and action as well as in theory. When he withdrew from the government on many occasions, and when he tried not to be a candidate for president in 1948, it was not because he didn't want to be the head of the government, nor because he didn't actually believe he could do a better job in that capacity than anybody else available. But it was because he believed that, due to internal political circumstances or world opinion, it would be better for China if he stepped aside. He was willing to sacrifice not only his own personal interests, but the more effective leadership which he knew he could offer, in order to avoid even the appearance of dictatorial interference with sound political development.

On the other hand, Chiang has believed that authority properly established must be unhesitatingly supported and obeyed. Otherwise every step won towards stability and permanence would be lost again. And he has emphatically insisted on the observance of that principle whenever and wherever it would properly apply. During the Sian incident he utterly amazed his captors by simply refusing to deal with them, or even talk with them, as man to man, at all. He took the strictly correct position that he was the head of the government, and they were rebels guilty of a treasonous action against that government; and that under these conditions there was absolutely no opening for negotiations and nothing to talk about. At this same time he gave one of many exhibitions of personal bravery, amounting almost to complete fearlessness, for which he is justly famous. He told his captors either to release him or to shoot him, as there was no other course. And he explained that if he died for the principles of the republic, his life would by that very act have become well worth while; but that, if his life were saved at the cost of concessions to his captors, then by that act it would cease to be worth the saving. And that was all he would say.

With Firmness When Needed . . .

Chiang can also be firm and severe when circumstances require it. During the Northern Expedition, when he had captured Nanking and had himself moved on, Communists controlling the Kuomintang government which had been set up in Hankow ordered and persuaded Chiang's Sixth Army Corps, which had been left behind, at Nanking, to loot the city and to commit outrages against the foreigners who were stationed there. Several foreigners were killed, and most of the four hundred in the city were saved only by the presence

177

and protection of British and American warships in the Yangtse River. Up to this point the revolutionary armies had had a completely unblemished record in their treatment of foreigners in China. Chiang was mortified to have this record broken, and determined that it should not happen again. As Commander-in-Chief he immediately took the blame for the whole affair, but simultaneously took swift action against those who had perpetrated it. Marching back to Nanking with troops he could safely trust, he isolated those which were under Communist officers, disarmed them, and had every soldier who had actually taken part in the outrages summarily executed. Then, learning that the Communists were planning to instigate an attack on the foreigners in Shanghai, where there were huge international settlements, Chiang moved before the Communists had a chance, put the city under martial law, and proceeded by a sizable number of arrests and executions to clear up that danger before it could erupt.

This summary action in Shanghai in 1927 has frequently been held up to view as the blackest spot in Chiang Kai-shek's career. And it is worth noting that at the time these unsparing preventive measures were taken Chiang had not yet become a convert to Christianity, for it is doubtful if he would have ever proceeded in quite the same way thereafter. Yet the Communists' real grievance was that he simply beat them to the punch, at their own game. Also it is worth noting that even in those early revolutionary days, when Chiang's discipline over any army he commanded was brutally strict, his humanitarian instincts were generous and sound. He enforced orders that any officer who retreated under fire would be shot; but he spent costly weeks capturing the city of Wuchang, which he could have taken in a day if he had been willing to bombard the civilian population.

Chiang Kai-shek speaks only Chinese. Except for his trips to Moscow in 1923, to India in 1942, and to Cairo during

178

World War II for the conference with Roosevelt and Churchill, he has never been out of eastern Asia. He has never become "westernized" as has, for instance, Syngman Rhee — or Madame Chiang. It is doubtful if Kipling would have picked him out as one who could "walk with kings, nor lose the common touch". But this is merely because his dignity is reinforced by a certain degree of oriental reserve. He is friendly and frank, without any touch of pompousness. His smile is infectious, his handshake firm. But he seems correctly aware that while to be a hail-fellow-well-met might be advantageous for an American politician, it would be neither proper nor becoming for the president of a nation of five hundred million people.

And Ready To Fight Again . . .

Besides personal courage Chiang has diplomatic courage, as shown when he demanded the recall of Stilwell during the war, or when he vetoed the admission of Mongolia to the United Nations only a year or two ago; and political courage, as has been shown on many occasions. He has originality, imagination, and the faculty of creative planning. He is a supremely skillful military commander, and a statesman in his follow-up of military gains. He has patience when it is needed, daring when it is called for, and realism among his mental lenses for appraising all situations. If the non-Communist world did not have a Chiang Kai-shek poised, ready to spring, on this side of the Formosa Strait, it would be difficult to invent his equal.

A Short Epilogue

It is now 1971. Please permit us, with the benefit of perhaps additional knowledge, once again to summarize very briefly the basic story that has been told so disjointedly in the preceding pages. Also to round out that story with an equally skeleton-like review of some relevant later events. And if there is much repetition for many readers in the first part of what follows, it is because we need that base to give strength to the second part.

It was in the fall of 1949 that Chiang Kai-shek fled from the mainland and established in Taipei, on the island of Taiwan, the seat of government of the Republic of China. He had been obliged, by war and revolution, to move his capital several times before. But this was a far more desparate and heroic venture. The combination of circumstances, and the massive success of incredibly evil forces, which compelled him to take this step, made it one of the greatest tragedies in human history.

All of his adult life it had been — and still is today — Chiang's unrelenting ambition to unify the whole of China into one great nation under a truly republican form of government. In following this dream he had to begin with the indescribable chaos that had been created by the Sun Yat-sen revolution during the decade following its outbreak in 1911. And by the time he reached any level of appreciable influence, the chaos was being converted into an even more horrible political morass by the effort of the Communists, trained in and directed from Moscow, to take over that revolution for Communist purposes.

This daring maneuver had begun as early as 1920. The first so-called Congress of the newly formed Chinese Communist Party, in 1921, was directed by a Dutchman named Maring, sent out from Russia to control the proceedings. A little later Earl Browder from the United States, Borodin from Russia, and other minions of Moscow arrived, to help to run the show. Their first objective was to seize control, from the inside, of Sun Yat-sen's great revolutionary party called the Kuomingtang. It was with this aim in mind that, as early as 1923, Li Ta-chao and Mao Tse-tung and some half a dozen other native Communists joined the Kuomingtang and in time got themselves elected to its Central Executive Committee.

The second objective of the Communists became to keep China divided until its unification could be accomplished by themselves, or with them in control. And their efforts along both lines became far more serious after Sun Yat-sen died early in 1925, at which time Chiang Kai-shek was only one of three or four potential heirs to Dr. Sun's influence and position. Nevertheless — to telescope this part of our narrative as tightly as we can — by 1927 Chiang had clearly established himself as Dr. Sun's successor. He had driven most of the native Communists out of the Kuomingtang, and drastically suppressed with military force their one serious effort to set up a Communist government. He had sent Browder, Borodin, and their leading foreign associates scurrying to Moscow. And through his famous "northern expedition" he had achieved at least a superficial unification between the political forces centered around Peking in the north, Shanghai in the center, and Canton in the south, of that vast stretch of China which borders on the Pacific Ocean.

But there was no end to the tasks and problems ahead.

One was to deal with the various warlords in all parts of the country. These were native "strong men" who had used the turmoil created by the revolution as a means and opportunity for making themselves regionally independent and immensely powerful. Some had already put themselves, at least theoretically, within the framework of Chiang's national government. Many had not. He now sought by negotiations if possible, by the threat of force if helpful, and by the actual use of force if necessary, to bring all of them and their domains into a legally unified China.

Chiang's successful concentration on this job, however, and on the other tremendous problems of organization and reconstruction by the first national government China had seen in sixteen years, required practically all of his strength and attention during 1928 through 1931. In the meantime the native Communists had also been extremely busy. With Mao Tse-tung taking the lead, under Stalin's blessing from Moscow, and with Chu Teh and Chou En-lai falling in line behind him, the Communists had embarked on the program of ruthless destruction and terror which they were to follow for the next two decades. They had already begun to develop sizable guerrilla bands, which Chiang had not been able to spare sufficient force to suppress.

For Mao and his followers had persuaded their bosses in Moscow to let them add a new facet to the abrasive tool called Communism. It was an adaptation to fit the realities of the China scene. Small progress could be expected from shouting to an industrial labor force the Marxian theme, *Workers of the world unite, you have nothing to lose but your chains!*, in a country where factories were so few and far between. So Mao's agitators, concentrating on the vast peasant population, had put their major effort into fomenting revolution — or the pretense thereof — under the slogan of "agrarian reform."

This vicious weapon of ruthless demagoguery had been

used by such ambitious Roman scoundrels as the Gracchi two thousand years before. But for the Mao gangsters it was never anything more than an ideological front, behind which they could employ more effective means of persuasion. By 1931 they were recruiting into their guerrilla "armies" the most foul, cruel, and cowardly elements of the population, through spreading arson, death, torture, and terror on a massive scale into several provinces. And before Chiang could do anything effective about it, a whole new factor of tremendous weight was thrown upon the scales.

For Japan, in the confident march of its increasingly aggressive imperialism, now decided to seize the vast northern Chinese province of Manchuria, and to grab off other parts of China in due course. This sinister plan got under way, on September 18, 1931, with an unprovoked attack on Mukden. At that very time (as the Japanese of course well knew) Chiang was in the midst of a determined military campaign to suppress the Communists, which was going very well. But he now felt obliged to send all of the armed force that he could to the north. And the Communists were given another respite.

Chiang, of course, was not able to save Manchuria. With a country that was not at all industrialized, that was poorly armed, and which was less than half recovered from such long years of disruption, he simply did not have the means to oppose the rising military might of Japan. Despite all he could do, the Japanese proceeded early in 1932 to convert Manchuria into their puppet state of Manchukuo. Also, in January of that year they began an attack on Shanghai which lasted for three months. They withdrew altogether from that effort in May. But in 1933 they overran the province of Jehol, on the border of Manchuria, and added it to the territory of Manchukuo. And from the very first assault on Mukden, the Chinese Communists had learned to synchronize their own activities with these successive moves by the

184

Japanese. This is why the very worst of their ineffably cruel and massive atrocities, in this period of their history, took place during 1932 and the first half of 1933.

By early in 1934, however, the dust of the Japanese invasions had settled for a while. And Chiang was able, at last, to turn his full strength and attention on the Communists. With rapid and decisive results. Government forces began to encircle and close in on their various guerrilla "armies." Many soon collapsed, and the remnants — always in civilian clothes and never in uniform, you must remember — had to sneak away if they could. By the end of 1934 Chiang had so completely routed them out of all of the provinces they had occupied that the straggling and struggling remainder of Mao's forces set out on their historic "long march."

This inglorious flight — later so bombastically glorified — was from Kiangsi Province in the southeast, on a circuitous route through mountainous areas to the west and then to the north, around to Yenan in the province of Shensi on the Mongolian border. Always on the run, marauding, murdering, burning, and gathering supplies as they went, this originally huge rabble took about two years and some five thousand miles to accomplish a move of less than a thousand miles. And there were only about five thousand armed Communists left when they did finally gather in the new headquarters that had been chosen for them by Moscow. In fact they were in such desperate straits that Mao and his followers decided to go through the motions of surrendering to the government, under the pretense that "The Kuomingtang and the Chinese Communist Party must cooperate to resist Japan and save the nation."

They made all kinds of promises, including one to obey Generalissimo Chiang Kai-shek's orders; another to abolish their "Red Army" and have it integrated into the National Army; and still another, to let their so-called "soviets" in

Shensi be reorganized into local governments. Chiang, desperate for all of the "unity" and help he could possibly get in the visibly forthcoming full-scale war with Japan, was patriotically foolish and forgiving enough to act on these promises. Instead of hanging these murdering traitors as they so richly deserved, in February 1937, his government began the necessary steps to reorganize the Chinese Communist force into the Eighth Route Army of the Chinese nation. Japan officially began the war by an attack against Shanghai on August 13, 1937. And before Chu Teh even led his Eighth Route Army out of northern Shensi Province for the first time, Mao Tse-tung made a speech to these troops, in which he said:

The Sino-Japanese War gives us, the Chinese Communists, an excellent opportunity for expansion. Our policy is to devote seventy percent of our effort to this end, twenty percent to coping with the Government, and ten percent to fighting the Japanese.

II

In the meantime Chiang had been consolidating his country and his government as well as he could, against all the tremendous odds of distance, chaos, poverty, and ignorance. There had never been any breathing spell at all. And now the Japanese War against China was to last for eight long years. By the time the United States was brought into this war in December, 1941, Japan had overrun the whole coastal border, and had in China an occupation force of military and civilian elements amounting to three million men. Chiang had been obliged to move his capital a thousand miles inland, to Chungking. And the peaceful rule of his country as a great republic seemed as far off as ever.

The bitter history of the next four years in China is fairly well known today. Immediately after Pearl Harbor Chiang had pledged to Roosevelt, on behalf of China, to give "all that we have and all that we are" to this fight against their common enemy. He lived up to that pledge in fullest measure. But the United States had been brought into the war by the deliberate cunning, perfidy, and treason of Franklin D. Roosevelt, George Marshall, and the Communists (or *Insiders* of the Great Conspiracy) who dominated Roosevelt's government. This was not because they had any interest in helping China, but as a means of putting American military and productive might at the service of Stalin. It was Japan that had attacked us, not Germany. Yet practically our whole effort was put into the war in Europe, while even MacArthur's forces in the Pacific were kept starved for supplies and handicapped as to moral support by hostile bureaucrats in Washington.

But what happened to our ally, Chiang Kai-shek, was even tremendously worse. We allowed his mortal enemies in our State Department to hamstring him in every way possible. We allowed the military supplies we did furnish this loyal and able ally to be doled out to him in the most humiliating fashion by such jealous and petty characters as "Vinegar Joe" Stilwell. We accepted the Yenan Communists as our trusted "allies," and insisted that Chiang Kai-shek treat them accordingly — even when they were keeping a very sizable part of Chiang's armies tied down in protecting his own people from the "allies." We ignored the Molotov-Matsuoka Pact, whereby Soviet Russia, for whom we were expending so much American blood and substance, remained for all practical purposes the ally of our enemy, Japan, and the enemy of our Chinese friends, throughout the whole war.

Roosevelt, with the direct help of Alger Hiss and other Communist agents, deliberately and brutally betrayed the interests of China at Yalta and other international conferences. Our government cold-bloodedly kept the war going in Asia for months after the Japanese were trying desperately to surrender — on exactly the same terms that were later accepted — because nothing could be more helpful to Stalin's diabolic intentions than this prolongation of the conflict in China. World War II was conducted by the United States Government, all over the earth and in every respect, for the benefit of the Communists, and of Stalin's plans for future imperialistic expansion of the Communist system. And nowhere did this policy have a more disastrous impact on the fortunes of our friends, or prove more advantageous to our most deadly enemies, than in China.

The time finally came, however, when V-J Day could not feasibly be postponed any longer. The war was declared over on August 15, 1945. Despite every handicap, insult, and betrayal, Chiang Kai-shek and his patriotic people had fought valiantly with us to the very end, and had contributed beyond any possible measurement to our combined victory over Japan. Chiang seemed at long last in position to move rapidly towards his unchanging goal of making all of China one great, peaceful, and prosperous republic. He should have been rewarded by the United States in every way for his tremendous loyalty as an ally, and supported by all appropriate means in his noble and patriotic ambition. Instead, the history of the next four years in China was even more bitterly tragic than had been the record of the preceding four.

The betrayal to which this great Christian statesman was now subjected by our government, and by the Communists who controlled Harry Truman, has seldom been equalled for foulness in the annals of our race. But Lenin had contended that, for Communism, the road from Moscow to Paris lay through Peking. Also, he had predicted that China would be the first of the great nations, after Russia, to fall into Communist hands. The *Insiders* of the international conspiracy had long seen in Chiang Kai-shek the one obstacle to their fulfillment of this guiding prophecy. At the end of the war in the Pacific these Conspirators had all of their plans in order and were sure that their time had come. And it is easy to list the factors and the measures by which Mao and Chou were thus enabled to impose their tyranny on the Chinese mainland.

(1) After eight years of grueling warfare both Chiang and China were exhausted. For the Communists, however, *their* war was still ahead. They had only been getting ready for it. And since 1942 they had been steadily building up their position and making their preparations with the unceasing help of the United States Government. They were our "allies," you understand!

(2) Immediately after V-J Day the Communists could — and did — abandon all pretense of being either subjects or allies of Chiang's government. They set out openly to attack, sabotage, and undermine it in every possible way. Their five thousand soldiers of 1937 had now grown to half a million guerrillas, which for the past three years the policies of *our* government had helped them to organize, train, and equip. So Mao and Chou already had the makings of their "Liberation Army" for carrying terror, destruction, and tyranny into one province after another. This they lost no time in undertaking. And by the end of 1945 Mao had at least a million people under his control.

(3) His allies back in the United States also lost no time. The glorification of Mao and his gang as idealistic and democratic "agrarian reformers," rather than regular Communists, had already been well launched by Edgar Snow in the *Saturday Evening Post*, and by other fabricators of fiction in the guise of fact. Both this theme, and the parallel stream of lies about Chiang and his government were now given tremendously greater impetus by a veritable flood of books and articles. The American people were rapidly conditioned to accept the downfall of Chiang, without realizing that he was actually being knocked down by ourselves.

(4) A major step by our government towards the destruc-

tion of Chiang Kai-shek was to disarm him. Large quantities of military supplies on the way to China when the war ended were actually destroyed enroute, to make sure that Chiang would not be able to use them against the Communists. In March, 1946 General George Marshall, who had arrived in China almost immediately after the war was over, with the full power of President Truman and Dean Acheson behind him, took a far more drastic step. He declared a complete embargo on the sale of any arms, ammunition, and replacements to National China, while boasting that he had thus disarmed thirty-nine of Chiang's divisions with a stroke of his pen. At the same time the policies of our government had led directly to the Soviets' seizure of Manchuria, and to their turning over to Mao's forces the vast stores of arms and ammunition which the Japanese had stockpiled in that province.

(5) Despite these handicaps Chiang's armies would still have been strong enough to wipe Mao's forces out of the areas they had overrun, and off the map of China, during the sixteen months between the end of the war and the end of 1946. For the training, arming, and grouping of these brigands did take time. And by December, 1946 the Communists had been pushed back from some of the boundaries they had reached and areas they had seized by the preceding January. But General Marshall was able to take care of that situation, as of many others. Every time the Chinese government forces had Mao's guerrilla armies on the run, Marshall brought enough pressure to bear on Chiang to compel him to accept a *truce* with the Communists, which gave them time to stave off defeat, regroup, and bring up some more supplies. There were three such truces imposed on Chiang by General Marshall, to save his Communist friends, during 1946 alone.

(6) At the same time Marshall was insisting that Chiang bring the Communist leaders into the Chinese Government.

Which would have been about like inviting professional embezzlers to become officers in a bank. But all of this top-level agitation on behalf of these Communist traitors, with the full prestige of the American Government behind Marshall's actions, did carry tremendous psychological weight in the Oriental mind. For one thing, it helped to persuade millions of the most intelligent but opportunistic Chinese that Mao — with the help of our government — was going to come out on top. And that therefore they had better abandon Chiang and try to get in the good graces of the Communists while they could. Which they no more realized to be utterly impossible for decent human beings than do Americans today.

(7) During all of this time, with Mao's guerrillas tearing up railroads, burning down warehouses, confiscating grain, and doing everything possible to wreck the economy of the country — after what eight years of war had already done — it was inevitable that increasingly wild inflation should begin to stalk the scene. What was needed, of course, was a sound and unshakable currency. But this was the last thing in the world that our pro-Communist State Department wanted to see provided for China at that time. And it successfully spiked every effort or even suggestion for creating such an aid to survival on which Chiang could depend.

(8) So inflation, disruption, disarmament, destruction, lies, sabotage, treason, and terror — all of them with the blessing of our State Department and its agents in China — took their continuous toll from the whole organization of Chinese life throughout 1947 and 1948. Until, in 1949, there came such an economic collapse, combined with the intended death blow delivered to Chiang by the State Department's *White Paper* full of falsehoods, that all defense on the mainland collapsed as well. And Chiang Kai-shek, determined to fight to the last ditch, led his battered forces and followers to the island which we once called Formosa, but now call Taiwan.

III

Those were incredibly dark days. Some two million refugees, with nothing left of their former homes and possessions, fled across the Formosa Strait in 1949 and 1950. A great many of them made this forty-eight hour trip, without food and water, in ships so crowded that men, women, and children even stood like sardines packed upright in the lavatories. And on the shore nothing awaited them — except freedom.

As the *American Legion Magazine* pointed out, in an excellent article in 1966, during the first six months that those refugees poured into Taiwan there were neither jobs nor food nor shelter for them, except what could be scrounged and improvised. "Huge squatter cities grew up, made of packing crates and odd bits of scrap metal and waste lumber. Former industrialists, government officials, business men, merchants and educators competed to pull rickshaws while Chiang and his top men tried to reorganize and settle the exiled government of China in its last remaining province."

The land all belonged to the six million native Taiwanese. Until 1945 these Chinese people had lived for fifty years as the subjects of Japan, in a conquered province. Taiwan had only been restored to China at the end of the war. Their economy was almost entirely dependent on primitive agriculture. There were no jobs in industry because there was practically no industry. Commercial activities were of small volume and elementary variety. The refugees were able to bring with them no tools, no equipment, extremely few possessions of any kind, and almost no industrial experience. And there was no telling when the well armed Communists might come over in pursuit.

Hindsight proves now that it was truly a magnificent concept of Chiang Kai-shek to withdraw to this small island province as a foothold. And to reestablish on it, despite all odds, the seat of his government, his legal authority as the duly elected President of the Republic of China, and the hopes of his countrymen for the future. But it bears repeating that these early months and even years were extremely difficult times for himself and his most faithful followers.

There were, however, many unseen forces at work which would in time prove all of this struggle and courage to be well worth while. Chief among them, sad to say, was a major policy decision by the enemy; that is, by the top *Insiders* of the Great Conspiracy, from whom Mao and Company took orders — as they still do today. As a basis for many longrange plans of the Conspiracy, these *Insiders* liked very much to set up *divided* countries. Such arrangements supplied them, far into the future, the means of bringing about the wars and conflicts on which their progress thrived.

Germany at the end of the war, Korea in 1948, Vietnam in 1954, were all deliberately divided for this purpose. The formula called for the United States to be officially and theoretically always on the side of the anti-Communist segment of the division — for *many* reasons. One was the planned ultimate effect, on the psychology and morale of the whole anti-Communist world, when it became clear just how unwilling or unable the United States was to keep these protégé domains from being subjected to terrific punishment by the Communists, or from eventually being brought under the Communist tyranny. And the Conspirators were quite willing to have China divided in accordance with this same formula. They grasped the advantages so quickly that Dean Acheson, for once in his life, was caught napping, and woke up to find that for a short distance he had been out of step with his bosses.

In the second place, there was arising in the United States at that very time such an awakening about the betrayal of eastern Europe *and* China into Communist hands, by our

193

government, and such a revulsion against it, as to make some ostensible huge steps backward by the Communists fit logically into their strategy. Having the United States Government shift over, therefore, and become for a few years a real friend and supporter of the anti-Communist Chiang Kai-shek — now that he was no longer dangerous — was a gambit that fitted beautifully into their game.

Everything fitted. It was the United States support of South Korea which made the Korean War possible, plausible, and such a vehicle for advancing Communist prestige and progress in Asia — and in the United States — precisely as had been planned. Exactly the same thing has been true, of course, with regard to South Vietnam and the war in southeast Asia. And there is no doubt that the ultimate betrayal of Chiang's government on Taiwan was also planned from the beginning, but with a much longer fuse.

This plan was merely dormant and on the shelf, even during the early 1950's, while our government was in general helping to strengthen the hands of the Republic of China, with Taipei as its temporary capital. For in 1965 all economic assistance was permanently discontinued. This real republic — as distinguished from The Peoples' Republic of China which the Communists call their tyranny on the mainland — was making far too much and too rapid progress in every way. Such a development clearly did not suit the plans of the *Insiders* who controlled the total show that was being enacted on the worldwide stage. And since that time the Taiwanese economic system has been entirely on its own.

For a third force had also been at work, almost from the day that Chiang first landed on the island. This force consisted of the tremendous patriotism, industriousness, and will to win of those who had sacrificed so much for freedom. Although very grateful for the American help that was soon being given them, and which at first was so desperately needed, Chiang and the Free Chinese set out to show what a free people, under honest

194

and honorable leadership, could accomplish for themselves. And it is the fantastic measure of their accomplishment, in so short a period as twenty years, starting from such almost hopeless conditions, that is the real theme of this epilogue. So let us now look — again briefly — at the record.

Perhaps we should start by remembering that Taiwan is almost exactly the size of Massachusetts and Connecticut combined, or one-fourth the size of North Carolina. And that in 1952, with the first great flood of refugees added, the population was a little over eight million. Today it is almost sixteen million. In area, therefore, the Province of Taiwan constitutes about two-fifths of one percent of China; in population, approximately two percent.

It was the end of 1952 before the refugees had become, even in the most superficial sense, settled and absorbed. The wild inflation, resulting from this addition of thirty-three percent to the native population and to the total demand for food, supplies, and services, had been brought under control, and a reasonably stable currency made available. Many other fundamental problems of government and of social organization had required — and received — at least pragmatic solutions, before any palpable progress could begin. We take 1952, therefore, as the starting point for most of our statistics and comparisons.

In 1952 the gross national product of Taiwan was just about exactly one billion dollars. Today it is approximately five billion dollars. And when conversion of these figures to constant values has been made, there has been a steady, cumulative, compounded average increase for the last decade of just about ten percent per year. This is despite the fact that *one-half* of the total population is under sixteen years of age; that a huge percentage of the potential labor force has necessarily been kept in a standing army of over half a million men; and that capital for industrial expansion has been a chronic need every step of the way.

195

The availability and use of electric power is universally considered an excellent index of economic progress. In 1952 the installed capacity in all of Taiwan amounted to only 300,000 kilowatts. By 1968 it had climbed to 1,940,000 kilowatts; by 1970 to 2,720,000. Despite this rapidly compounded growth, demand has run constantly far beyond the supply. The present expectation and plans have been that by 1983 the installed capacity would amount to over 8,000,000 kilowatts. And the Taiwanese have had a superb habit of steadily surpassing all such projections.

By 1960 Taiwan was already becoming an exporting country of growing significance. And not just in raw or processed agricultural products, but in manufactured items of increasing complexity and sophistication. Growing industries included the manufacture of rubber tires and tubes, cement, plywood, rayon, glass, pharmaceuticals and other chemical products, household appliances, and machinery. Since then there have been *many* additions to this list, especially including electronics. Not only has Taiwan already become one of the leading electronics manufacturing centers in all of the Far East; but, because of the very honorable and dependable treatment given foreign investors in the Taiwanese economy, there have already been more than fifty electronics plants established on the island by foreign capital.

The most amazing part of this whole economic picture, in fact, is the manner in which these developments, just getting under way in 1960, have been so rapidly and phenomenally expanded. Or, more precisely, the extent to which this isolated and tight little island, with its extremely hardworking people, and with all of the freedoms and incentives in an honorably run republic, has made of itself, in so short a time and from so small a base, one of the important exporting areas of the world. Its total foreign trade for 1970 consisted of $1,545 million in exports and $1,505 million in imports, showing a trade balance in its favor of forty million dollars.

And the total, both ways, of three billion and fifty million dollars showed an increase over the preceding year of 735 million dollars!

For 1971 the forecast is four billion dollars (or an increase of one billion dollars over 1970!), with an unfavorable trade balance of sixty million. The estimate for 1973 is six billion dollars. This would go far ahead of all the foreign trade (including opium!) of the whole Communist empire on the mainland, with its seven hundred million inhabitants. In fact the 1971 total will probably surpass, or just about equal, that of the Communist domain with some fifty times as much population. Or, put in another light, the *per capita* foreign trade of Taiwan even in 1970 was $213 per year, compared with $5.60 (!) per year in the domain ruled by the Communists just across the Formosa Strait.

Let's pick up one more set of very impressive — and entirely reliable — statistics. During the last decade, 1960-1970, the national income of Taiwan was multiplied by 3.35 and — again despite the immense population growth, and number of children involved — the per capita income was multiplied by 2.56! Because of such strong industrial growth, agriculture's share of the total national production declined during this period from over thirty percent to less than twenty percent, but there was still plenty of food for everybody, as we shall see.

When we turn from the material to the spiritual side of life, and take a look at education as the most convenient criterion, we find that the achievements of Chiang's government and people have been equally impressive. Their educational system begins with free compulsory education for six years in the primary schools, starting for each pupil at the age of six. In the 1968-1969 period there were 2,244 of these schools, with an average attendance of a little over one thousand children each, making a total enrollment of 2,383,204. This was 97.7 percent of the population of that age.

The next stage consists of junior and senior high schools of three years each. Attendance is not compulsory, but has been rapidly growing. In this same 1968-1969 year, the number of elementary school graduates going on to these secondary schools was 73.3 percent, or 770,102 students. This was an increase of 129,655 students — requiring an addition of 206 such schools — over 1967-1968. And 67.4 percent of the graduates of these secondary schools then go on to college. You can readily see why, already, twice as large a percentage of Taiwanese youngsters receive college educations as do their counterparts in England.

In 1969 there were eighty-five universities, colleges, and junior colleges on Taiwan. Seven were run by the national government, nineteen by regional government bodies, three by municipalities, and fifty-six were private institutions. Enrollment during that year reached 161,337, which was an increase of 22,724 over the preceding academic year. A uniform entrance examination is held annually under joint sponsorship of both the public and private colleges. That it is no sinecure or mere formality is shown by the fact that, in 1968, only 23,313 out of 68,930 applicants passed this examination.

The current emphasis is on the establishment and expansion of graduate schools. In 1968-1969 there were 110 such facilities for postgraduate work, which showed a gain of twenty-one over the preceding year. It should be noted also that this was a larger number than that of the academies for undergraduates. But of course the attendance in each of these specialized institutions was far smaller. They simply show the tremendous interest, on the part of Taiwanese youth, in higher or professional studies in mathematics, physics, chemistry, biology, and engineering.

There is less interest, it seems, in advanced scholarship in literature and the liberal arts, even though the government is awarding prizes and giving scholarships for superior work in

198

the field of traditional Chinese culture. But "one must eat before one can philosophize," and these people are under immense practical pressures in a utilitarian and pragmatic world. So they can't have everything. And what they have been building for themselves is almost beyond belief when you know the whole background of their undertaking.

But we cannot spare the time and space to make this sampling of our subject more extensive or comprehensive. So we must omit many areas of remarkable progress by the *Republic of China* which deserves tremendous acclaim. And we give you instead just a few extremely miscellaneous reports that seem to us revealing and significant, as well as of rather strong human interest. One is simply a report by the United Nations that, by 1966, the people in Taiwan had become the best fed in all of Asia. The second is that, by unquestionable statistics, the lifespan of the people of Taiwan has increased remarkably during the past twenty years. In 1950 the expectation for men was 52.9 years and that of women 56.4 years. As of 1969 the figures were 65.1 years for men and 70.8 years for women! Obviously, among the other benefits of hard work, long hours, individual freedom, honorable dealings, and the desire to "get ahead," is the fact that it makes you live longer. Or it certainly has amid all the glorious hopes for the future in the Republic of China.

Of lesser importance but still worth mentioning, if we had the room and you had the patience, are a hundred items like the following. The Southern Cross-Island Highway, third in a series of beautiful and extensive automobile roads — some of which require major feats of engineering — was recently completed *six months ahead of schedule*! Can you remember *any* government job carried out in our *republic* which was even finished on time? Second is the fact that the Taiwan universities and colleges are not infested with hippies and revolutionaries. Practically all students who attend those institutions, being very grateful for the opportunity to acquire a college education, go there in order to learn something instead of to make a militant exhibition of their ignorance.

Related to the last point is the rather astounding circumstance that the city of Taipei, with nearly two million inhabitants, has a police force of only four thousand regulars and two thousand volunteers. With a total annual budget of only five million dollars! And any man, or any woman, can walk the streets of Taipei, or of any other city on Taiwan, at any hour of day or night, with confidence and safety. Also, please note the further fact that in Taipei, or on all of Taiwan, you do not find any beggars (except for outright crooks who prey primarily on American servicemen). The whole Republic of China offers convincing evidence that where people are really willing to work, and the government does not clog the operation of economic laws, beggary as a profession is neither necessary nor profitable.

Beggary is out of place in a pioneer setting. And we have in the Republic of China today some very positive proof that the pioneer spirit of a people does not depend on, nor require, vast open spaces. The population per square mile of Taipei is just about twice that of New York City. Of Taiwan as a whole it is approximately three times that of New York State. Yet Chiang Kai-shek, and his thousands of like-minded subordinates, and the fifteen million free Chinese on Taiwan today, are very determined pioneers in the best meaning of that inspiring word. They are striking out with tremendous energy, enthusiasm, boldness, and success on what are to them entirely new paths of knowledge, of technological progress, of commercial and industrial greatness, of scientific exploration, and of practical solutions to man's political and sociological problems.

It is the constant hope and resolution of these Chinese patriots to transport to the mainland the knowledge, the spirit, and the accomplishments which are already transforming Taiwan. And to use what they have so happily achieved

200

under freedom — while all the rest of their country was being reduced to festering despair under tyranny — as a basis and a beginning for making all of China a wonderfully free, prosperous, and happy nation. But there are ominous signs today that their dream is to be turned into a nightmare, through no fault of their own and by forces utterly beyond their present power to oppose. These brave pioneers on behalf of a better world are now in imminent danger of being themselves brought under the merciless brutality of the beasts in Peking.

At the time this book is being published and this epilogue written, initial steps toward the sellout of Taiwan are already under way. Others are visibly being planned which go a great deal further. For the last few years the Red Tyranny in China, living through internecine strife of vicious and massive proportions, has existed on the very edge of being toppled by its own colossal crimes, schisms, and failures. Once again it is to be saved by the strategic support of the United States Government, as has happened on so many earlier occasions for both the Peking and the Moscow regimes.

But this time there seems to be far more contemplated by Washington than merely some defensive assistance to a friend in trouble. Both words and actions by the Nixon Administration already indicate that all the prestige, power, and resources of the United States may be placed behind some forthcoming pressures to give the Chinese Communists undisputed hegemony over all of eastern Asia. And that in any event one of the earliest steps in this gigantic buildup of our worst enemies — namely Mao Tse-tung and Chou En-lai — will consist of sacrificing to them our best friends, namely Chiang Kai-shek and his anti-Communist supporters.

Once before, in the years 1944 through 1949, Chiang and his people were completely and almost fatally betrayed by our government. Now they are threatened with an even more perfidious and drastically final betrayal by this same false friend. It will be an eternal disgrace to us, the American people, if we allow this treachery to be carried out. We shall have even more heartrending reasons to cry to Heaven itself — Again, May God Forgive Us!

Index